Hoodoo Shrines and Altars
Sacred Spaces in Conjure and Rootwork

Miss Phoenix LeFae

Missionary Independent Spiritual Church
Forestville, California

→ 2015 ←

Hoodoo Shrines and Altars:
Sacred Spaces in Conjure and Rootwork
by Miss Phoenix LeFae

© 2015 Phoenix LeFae
PhoenixLeFae.com

All rights reserved under International and Pan-American Copyright Conventions. No part of this publication can be reproduced, stored in a retrieval system, or transmitted in any format by any means, electronic, mechanical, photocopying, recording, or otherwise, without the written permission of the copyright owner.

Some material in this book appeared at these webs sites and is used with permission:
Association of Independent Readers and Rootworkers
ReadersAndRootworkers.org
ReadersAndRootworkers.org/wiki/Category:Altar_Work_And_Prayers
Lucky Mojo Curio Company Forum
Forum.LuckyMojo.com
Forum.LuckyMojo.com/altars-questions-and-answers-t124.html

Text:
Phoenix LeFae

Editor:
catherine yronwode, Charles Porterfield, nagasiva yronwode

Cover:
Greywolf Townsend, Unknown "Retro" Vector Artis

Production:
catherine yronwode, nagasiva yronwode

Illustration:
Charles C. Dawson, Steve Leialoha, Greywolf Townsend

First Edition 2015
Second Edition 2017

Published by
Missionary Independent Spiritual Church
6632 Covey Road
Forestville, California 95436
MissionaryIndependent.org

ISBN: 978-0-9960523-3-7

Printed in Canada.

Contents

Dedication 4
Acknowledgements 4
Altars of the Ancestors
    Hoodoo: A Brief Introduction 5
    How Do We Know About Hoodoo Altars? 6
    Altar Described by Helen Pitkin 8
    Altars Described by Zora Neale Hurston 9
    Altars Described to Harry M. Hyatt 10
    Altar Described by Mikhail Strabo 14
    Altars Described by Henri Gamache 15
"You Shall Build There an Altar"
    Definition of Altars 16
    Basic Types of Altars 18
    Altar Work or Just Work? 21
    Altars for What Purpose? 22
    Building the Altar 23
    Practical Altar Tips 28
    Altar Paraphernalia 29
    Magical and Spiritual Correspondences 39
    Cleaning and Maintaining the Altar 43
    Altars for Ongoing Work 49
    Cat Yronwode's Secrets of Altar Respect 50
Altars for Various Conditions
    Altars for Love 54
    Altars for Money 56
    Altars for Healing 58
    Altars for Protection 60
    Altars for Justified Enemy Works 61
    Altars for Cursing and Vengeance 62
Shrines of Veneration
    Ancestors Altars 63
    Altars for Catholic Saints 65
    Making Offerings to Spirits 66
Unusual Altars
    Travelling Altars 67
    Pocket Shrines 69
    Hidden Altars 72
    Business and Office Altars 76
    Candle Ministry Altars 79
Frequently Asked Questions 80

Dedication

I am dedicating these pages to the ancestors of the hoodoo tradition; to all of those conjure workers, root doctors, and spiritual practitioners who kept this magic alive; to those folks who worked for the betterment of their communities as healers of mind, body, and spirit; and to all of those who knew that the key to helping future generations was to pass their knowledge along. The world is a richer place because of their dedication to us.

Acknowledgements

This book has been a work in progress for a couple of years, and I am so excited to see it finally come to life.

I want to acknowledge and thank my darling husband Gwion who has been a constant support to me. He has encouraged me more than any other person on the planet, even when I resisted. Thank you is not enough; you are a dear and I appreciate you so very much. A special thanks to my kids, Trinity and Amy, for the many nights I was unavailable because I was writing away.

Thanks to my amazingly talented and wonderful co-workers at Missionary Independent Spiritual Church and the Lucky Mojo Curio Company next door: Katrina, Lupita, Shenique, Yosé, Heidi, Leslie, Eileen, Nikki, Ernie, Dave, Brian, Bo, Alicia, Angela, and others who have come and gone. These are the folks with whom I spend most of my time every week, and if it wasn't for their support, encouragement, amusement and hilarity right when I need it, I might not have made it this far.

A huge thank you and a tip of my hat to Catherine Yronwode. Meeting you and learning from you has transformed my life and made much of what I've dreamt of possible. You have taught me more about life than you could possibly know. Thanks also to Nagasiva Yronwode for his constant grace and patience and to Charles Porterfield, Khi Armand, Greywolf Townsend, and the others who have contributed ideas, information, expertise, and their time.

And last, but not least, my thanks go out to those folks in the Association of Independent Readers and Rootworkers who made me feel like part of the team, even when I technically wasn't, and welcomed me in when I did join: Elvyra Love, Lou Florez, Deacon Millett, ConjureMan Ali, and Ms. Melanie; hugs all around.

Altars of the Ancestors

HOODOO: A BRIEF INTRODUCTION

WHAT HOODOO IS

Hoodoo, also called conjure, rootwork, helping yourself, throwing roots, and tricking, is a folkloric magical, spiritual, and healing tradition of African-Americans, the descendants of African slaves. It is found all over the United States, wherever Black Americans live.

The aim of hoodoo is to increase luck, remove evil, and achieve various desires. Practitioners utilize a specific repertoire of magical items, such as roots, minerals, mojo bags, dressing oils, powders, and candles, and they favour a certain range of techniques, including foot-track magic, bathing, floor washing, Christian prayer, moving candle spells, and the setting of lights. Much of the work is done at home, but professional root doctors also exist who will undertake jobs on behalf of clients.

During its early history, hoodoo was transmitted orally within small rural communities. In the late 19th century, audio recordings, mass literacy campaigns, and the urbanization of the nation's population brought about changes in how this was transmitted. By the 1920s, Black music was distributed via radio and records, and hoodoo was being written down and marketed by mail order, even as its practitioners reached out to incorporate new ways of working. Native herbal healers, German and Scots-Irish spell-casters, and Jewish pharmacists have all played small parts in the making of contemporary hoodoo, but it remains, as ever, the magic of Black Americans.

Here are a few sources to learn more about the history of hoodoo:
LuckyMojo.com/hoodoohistory.html
Southern-Spirits.com

WHAT HOODOO IS NOT

Hoodoo has strong Christian spiritual components, but it is not a religion. You do not have to be an initiate to practice it. There isn't a secret handshake, a special ritual, or a hidden exotic temple to enter before you can learn how to do it. Hoodoo grew out of the African Diaspora, but it is not Vodou, Santeria, Palo, Lukumí, or Sanse. It is also not Satanism or Devil Worship. The primary language spoken in hoodoo is English, and the Lord served is the God of Abraham, Isaac, and Jacob, and His beloved son, Jesus Christ.

HOW DO WE KNOW ABOUT HOODOO ALTARS?

If hoodoo started as a rural oral tradition, handed down through family and community lines, how did hoodoo arrive on the world stage? If it was once a secret system, how did it get brought out into the open?

Well, in the first place, conjure never was very "secret." It was simply ignored or scorned by the White over-culture. Thankfully, Black conjure workers have shared their knowledge via printed texts or by talking to folklorists and scholars. Because of their generous information sharing, we know quite a lot about hoodoo's history — and need not make it a mystery.

These are not the only sources for our knowledge, but they are good ones:

EX-SLAVE NARRATIVES

Before Emancipation in 1863, many Black slaves who escaped northward wrote memoirs. Their mentions of hoodoo show how conjure doctors worked at that time. In the 1930s, as the last of America's ex-slaves were passing away, the U.S. government funded a state-by-state series called *Slave Narratives: A Folk History of Slavery in the United States From Interviews with Former Slaves*, prepared by the Federal Writers' Project of the Works Progress Administration. These also teach us about Black magical culture.

You can read ex-slave narratives that describe hoodoo online here:
Southern-Spirits.com

MISS ALICE BACON AND MISS LEONORA HERRON

In 1895 these women at the all-Black Hampton Institution (now Hampton University) in Virginia collected conjure lore from the students and published it in *The Southern Workman and Hampton School Record*. Their series, "Folklore and Ethnology: Conjuring and Conjure Doctors in the Southern United States," was reprinted in the *Journal of American Folklore*, and was the first notice many White scholars had that hoodoo even existed.

NEWBELL NILES PUCKETT AND HELEN PITKIN

A White folklorist born in Mississippi, Puckett interviewed 400 Black conjure practitioners for *Folk Beliefs of the Southern Negro,* published in 1926. His *Names of American Negro Slaves* (1937) is a study of African name retentions by 19th century American slaves. He also reprinted descriptions of New Orleans conjure documented by Helen Pitkin in 1904.

ZORA NEALE HURSTON

Ms. Hurston was an African-American folklorist and novelist who published over 50 stories, plays, and essays based on her experiences, among them *Their Eyes Were Watching God, Dust Tracks On a Road, Sweat, Jonah's Gourd Vine, Tell My Horse,* and *Moses, Man of the Mountain.* Her book on hoodoo, *Mules and Men,* was published in 1935.

HARRY M. HYATT

Reverend Hyatt was an Anglican minister and a dedicated folklorist. For 35 years, from 1935 to 1970, he interviewed 1,600 African-American practitioners in 13 states about rootwork and conjure. The hoodoo spells he collected — more than 13,400 of them — were published in his books *Folklore From Adams County Illinois (1935)* and *Hoodoo - Conjuration - Witchcraft - Rootwork* (5 volumes, 1970 - 1978).

You can read more about Harry M. Hyatt and his 1,600 informants here:
LuckyMojo.com/hyatt.html
LuckyMojo.com/hyattinformants.html

MIKHAIL STRABO

Mikhail Strabo is the pseudonym of Sydney J. R. Steiner, a Jewish author in the 1940s who worked with Black associates to document Spiritual Church practices in books like *The Guiding Light to Power and Success, How to Conduct a Candle Light Service, The Magic Formula for Successful Prayer,* and *The Magic Formula for Personal Power.*

You can read more about Mikhail Strabo online here:
LuckyMojo.com/strabo.html
Strabo's drawings of the altars of Rev. Adele Clemons are here:
"The Art of Hoodoo Candle Magic" by C. Yronwode and M. Strabo

HENRI GAMACHE

Henri Gamache is the pseudonym of Joseph Spitalnick, a.k.a. Joe Kay, but later identified by Kay's son Ed as a "female Jewish college student" of the 1940s. Gamache wrote *The Master Book of Candle Burning,* as well as other hoodoo classics like *The Magic of Herbs, Terrors of the Evil Eye Exposed,* and *The Mystery of the Long Lost 8th, 9th, and 10th Books of Moses.*

You can read more about the mysterious Henri Gamache online here:
LuckyMojo.com/young.html

ALTARS DESCRIBED BY ZORA NEALE HURSTON

"Folklore is not as easy to collect as it sounds. The best source is where there are the least outside influences and these people, being usually under-privileged, are the shyest."

— Zora Neale Hurston

Having defined a few terms and made a few distinctions among the various types of altars found in hoodoo, let us now turn to the history of altars in Black-American magic. Rather than speak from personal gnosis or take on an unsuitable air of authority, we will begin with first-hand accounts of what hoodoo altars have actually looked like in the past.

The following information comes from interviews conducted by the African-American folklorist and novelist Zora Neale Hurston and published in her 1935 book *Mules and Men,* based upon material she collected in Florida and Louisiana from 1927 to 1929.

A MEMORY OF MARIE LAVEAU'S ALTAR-HELPERS

"The ones around her altar fix everything for the feast. But nobody see Marie Laveau for nine days before the feast. But then the great crowd of people at the feast call upon her, she would rise out of the waters of the lake with a great communion candle burning upon her head and another in each one of her hands."

— Luke Turner, New Orleans, La., circa 1928.

A CURSING ALTAR FOR DEATH-WORK

"She set the altar for the curse with black candles that have been dressed in vinegar. She would write the name of the person to be cursed on the candle with a needle. Then she place fifteen cents in the lap of Death upon the altar to pay the spirit to obey her orders."

— Luke Turner, New Orleans, La., circa 1928.

BRAIN CORAL FOR DOMINATING MENTAL POWER

"'Only thing that's holding me here is this.' She pointed to a large piece of brain coral that was forever in a holy spot on the altar. 'That's where his power is.'"

— Mary Watson, New Orleans, La., circa 1928.

AN ALTAR DESCRIBED BY HELEN PITKIN

An Angel by Brevet: A Story of Modern New Orleans by Helen Pitkin was published in 1904 as fiction, but 20 years later the novel was cited by Newbell Niles Puckett as source material. He said that, "although written in the form of fiction, [Pitkin] assures me, personally, that [the scenes described] are scientifically accurate, being an exact reproduction of what she herself has seen or obtained from her servants and absolutely free from imagination." What follows is Deacon Millett's summary of the altar work, extracted from his book *"Hoodoo Return and Reconciliation Spells."*

Angelique, the heroine of the book, has a rival in love and resorts to visiting conjuror Madame Peggy for aid. "Angele now suffered the most strenuous embarrassment she had ever known. 'I love where I am not loved in return,' she said in a hard voice." She is asked to remove all her black clothing. "Nothing must be crossed, neither your feet, neither your hands. For fear two pins might cross in your hair, it is best to take them out now."

An altar of fruit, candies, and alcohol is on the floor. "In the center a saucer was set, in which were white sand, quicksilver, and molasses, apexed by a blue candle … On the hearth were the outlines of a large black pot, from which there was the whisper of a simmer and a luscious steam."

In the ceremony that follows, we see hoodoo touches: Angele must write her own name, her lover's, and her rival's on slips of paper. The slip with her rival's name is placed to soak in a dish of vinegar, salt, and Pepper; the name papers of herself and her beloved dropped into a bowl of burning whiskey "that sent leaping shadows into the dark corners."

"Ma'm Peggy lifted the candles from the altar … and handed one to Angele. It bore seven notches in the blue tallow, and Ma'm Peggy instructed her to burn it seven nights in her own bedroom, only from notch to notch, repeating three Hail Mary's. The sorceress then gave Angele a pinch of the poiv' guine [Guinea Grains] from the saucer and bade her put five grains in her mouth whenever her lover would come near her, this to soften him towards her; also, when he would first enter the house, to make a glass of sugared water, very sweet, and with basilique [Basil], and throw it in the yard with her back towards the street."

Here we see a hoodoo candle altar on the floor; a reference to crossed conditions; the use of name papers, whiskey, herbs, and vinegar; and a home-made 7-knob candle for a client to set at home to back up the work.

ALTARS DESCRIBED TO HARRY M. HYATT

The following information on altars is drawn from the interviews gathered by Reverend Harry M. Hyatt between 1936 and 1970. This is just a sampling of the information he collected and published in the five volumes of *Hoodoo-Conjuration-Witchcraft-Rootwork*. Hyatt recorded his interviews on wax cylinders and they were later written out by hired transcriptionists in phonetic spelling. However, for ease of reading, they have been rewritten here in conventional spelling. The words in parentheses are those of Hyatt asking questions. The names of the informants are given where known, but many informant names were lost, and only their numbers and locations remain. The numbers in parentheses are Hyatt's recording cylinder numbers.

HIDDEN CANDLE ALTAR IN "A SPECIAL CORNER"
(Where would you set that [black] candle [to make folks leave town]?)
"Well, I would set it in a special corner ... in a corner where a chiffarobe is at or anything to hide it to keep the other people from seeing it."
(You have an office. And do you have a room with an altar or something of that sort?)
"I has an altar."
(Do you dress in any special way?) [A Spiritualist minister, he was wearing a business suit and carrying a briefcase when interviewed.]
"I dress different ways. I got robes I dress in."
— Doctor Caffrey #840, New Orleans, La., (1263 - 1270), page 1459.

CLEAN ALTAR SPACES
(Have you ever heard of people having little altars?)
"Yes, I do that myself. We have our altar and we have the holy oil because everything must be holy. And because it's a place, people are coming and cursing and that, and sometimes they'll forget and so the place is full of evil and dirty. But everything must be clean. You have seven holy candles, large ones, but you place them in the form of a cross. If you don't have those candlesticks that form the cross, why, you can just set your candles in a row ... then you burn your incense. We call it holy incense and you then use holy water ... pray the 23rd Psalm."
— Informant #627, Washington, D.C. (802:5 - 803:2), page 748.

LITTLE LIGHTS BURNING
"I was kind of down and out and that's why I went there to see them and they told me what candles to light. Sometimes they tell me to put a light."
(What did you see when you went into the room?)
"What did I see when I went into the room? Well, the room was dark and I could see these little lights burning. There are light burning at the altar."
(What was the person wearing?)
"[…] A lavender robe with a silver and lavender crown on their head."
(Then, were you supposed to do anything when you came in or went out?)
"Yes, I make the sign of the cross and get down on my knees and go to the altar and pray to the saint to do things for me."
— #791, New Orleans, La., (1111:3), page 770.

PRAYING AT THE ALTAR
"Yes sir, they still have altars over there. You go in and the altar is just sitting there like on a vanity or bureau and the candles are always lit. You get down on your knees and you pray. Whatever prayer, whatever you want done, you pray and that saint will help you, understand? You pray to that saint.
"Then you go to the mother of that church. She will come to you and she may give you a medal. She'd bless the medal and pray over it. Then she would tell you what to do and how to do it…."
— #832, New Orleans, La., (1245:2), page 772.

CANDLES ON THE ALTAR
"The altar is a table and on it she's got all different candles, you know, the table is shaped like a pulpit. They have all different kinds of candles, white candles, green candles, they got pink ones, they got red ones…."
— #783, New Orleans, La., (1089:2), page 772.

"SHE HAD A KEY"
"The room had candles and it had an altar. They had about 20 different candles; some red, some blue, black, and green."
(Anything on the walls?)
"No, they didn't have anything on the walls…She had a hat, like a cap on, a silk cap and a big robe. It was a purple robe with a big key — a chain with a big key, like the old-time door key, hanging in front of her."
— #782, New Orleans, La., (1083:1), page 780.

HOW MYRTLE COLLINS WORKED FOR CLIENTS

Myrtle Collins of Memphis, Tennessee, was a Rosicrucian and a spiritual doctor. Hyatt interviewed her twice, in 1938 and 1939. She told him how she worked, whom she served, and how her altar was set up in her home.

(Do you have a special room set aside for your altar?)

"Yes sir. No one goes in that room but myself and the people I tell,"

(What does it look like?)

"It's an ordinary altar, like a church altar ... I use a white satin [altar cloth] with white satin fringe. ... I have three baskets that sit on top of the [supply] cabinet to catch evil spirits. There's a prayer that you say to consecrate that when you put them up there."

"In that room I wear white robes. I wear a white satin hat. It's a cap-like. It just fits your head. That cap is worn for [spiritual] protection."

[For a prostitute]: "You use Saint Raymond ... because he's for hustling women and you would set two red tapers for him ... put his picture right up over the altar. The woman would be in the same room with me, on her knees, praying for the type of life she leads ... to pull men in and get money."

[For a death spell]: "For someone that injured you and you wanted them to die, you would burn two black taper candles, or two black candles and one red one if they are to be accidentally killed. But just to take their strength and make their heart fail, you use only black candles. They fade away."

[For safe travel]: "I would offer you up to Saint Peter, for Peter walked the sea. I would offer prayer that you not lose your faith ... two white candles."

(Do you ever use holy water?)

"Yes, sir. I use holy water to obtain strength and luck, success and happiness. Bathe the face, look toward the east, and recite the Lord's Prayer."

(You bathe the patient's face with it?)

"Yes, sir. Or let them bathe with it. I've never had to bathe a man, but I have bathed women. I have a white basin, and I bathe the body down with a sponge in that formula [a mineral or herbal preparation]."

(Where do you get your holy water? You consecrate it?)

"I consecrate my holy water myself, in the name of the Father and the son ... I bless it at 12 o'clock midnight. I always have some on hand."

[By her second interview, Collins had bought a farm near San Jose, California. She ordered supplies from New York, Chicago, and Mississippi.]

— Myrtle Collins, #926 / 1538, Memphis, Tennessee (1503-1509 / 2779-2793), page 992.

SAINTS ON THE ALTAR
"But you have Saint Peter's picture, you stand up to the altar and you are going to roll, you move, and roll over it and when you get there you grab the altar and you say your wish."
— Doctor Caffrey, #840, New Orleans, La., (1263 - 1270), page 1459.

DRESS OF THE ALTAR WORKER
"Most of them dress in a gown — sometimes it's a black gown. If you are doing work to hurt somebody it is a black gown. If you go there for gambling it is a green or a pink one. But most of the time when you go in there they have a black gown on. He sits in front of the altar. On the altar there are all kinds of candles and saints of all kinds. And you just tell him what you want him to do and how you want him to do it. He sets that candle to that saint."
— Hoodoo Book Man, #786, New Orleans, La., (1091-1097), page 1754.

PROFESSOR FRANK'S RED ALTAR ROOM
"Professor Frank came out all dressed in a very gorgeous robe, seemingly made of red velvet with large arms. He had a cap on, the same as that which a priest wears, and he told the man to come and kneel.

"The room was lighted with two large candles on either side of a mantelpiece, red candles. The carpet on the floor was red, and then they had a large altar over in the corner. It seemed to set the room off katty-cornered, and there was a stool by which a man could kneel down upon as the people do in some of the churches to pray. The front of the altar was of a deep dark red velvet with fringe all the way around and it was worked with gold and various colours of stars and moons. It had a large gold and silver horseshoe mingled with seemingly various colours and ivory.

"This man knelt down on this stool and he told him to put his right hand on his heart and his left hand on a book which was supposed to be the Sixth and Seventh Books of Moses of witchcraft and superstition.

"On a side table there was a large red covering, with fringe. There was a large reading lamp with the shade seemingly of gold. Professor Frank went behind the table and sat down in a large reclining revolving chair. But before he sat down in the chair, he pulled out a kind of pipe. It was gold and it had a little crooked pipe stem to it."
— Rev. Young, New Orleans, La., (# lost) (cylinder # lost), page 129.

ALTAR DESCRIBED BY MIKHAIL STRABO

"If your meeting room does not have a permanent pulpit in the front center of the platform, we suggest that you place a large oblong table there. If your meeting room has something that cannot or should not be moved, set your table to the right of this object. In the center of the table set your large candle or Master candle, as we shall call it, in a suitable holder or on a large plate. Then arrange for several other holders or plates to be available for the use of the members of your group. It is the custom in some churches to use white plates of heavy, white restaurant-ware.

"If possible get a large slab of some fireproof material, such as granite or marble, large enough to cover the entire table. This will eliminate the need for plates or holders, as the candles can then be placed directly on this fireproof material. As a further suggestion you might use a large shallow metal container which can be filled with bright, clean sand. Your candles can then be placed upright in the sand. However, as you read further, you may see reasons why you may prefer the use of plates for certain types of services, under certain conditions.

"Around the large Master candle set a few smaller candles. We suggest that you do not put out all that you have, but rather keep a supply in reserve, and easily accessible, in a plain, unmarked metal or wooden box.

"Some celebrants use various adjuncts on their tables or altars. Some use burning incense in a brazier, others use flowers in vases or baskets, others use one or two seven-branched candlesticks. You can, according to your requirements, use any or all of these things.

"If you use a reading stand, put it to one side. You should not conduct your service from in front of the candles.

"Now let us proceed to the actual service.

"When you are prepared to open your service, and after the group has been seated, have the room darkened. It is preferable to have all the lights in the room extinguished. Then, as your congregation sits silently in the darkness, the music can begin.

"It is best to use some simple music, simple enough to be played in the dark by your organist, or some pre-recorded selections that can be obtained from any store where recorded music is sold."

For more 1940s altars by Mikhail Strabo see:
"The Art of Hoodoo Candle Magic" by C. Yronwode and M. Strabo

ALTARS DESCRIBED BY HENRI GAMACHE

The following information on altars is drawn from Henri Gamache's 1942 book *The Master Book of Candle Burning,* which remains the most influential text on candle magic in the conjure tradition. Its contents range from beautifully benevolent spells for blessing and healing to truly hateful spells of anger. Gamache's spells and altar work typically feature carefully selected and placed candles in symbolic colours, dressed with named condition oils. They also include the reading of Psalms from a Bible kept open upon the altar.

ALTAR AND CANDLE STICKS IN THE PHILOSOPHY OF FIRE

"In the beginning, the altar was the one place where primitive man could meet with God. He felt that he could not just offer up a sacrifice at any place that he might happen to be. He had to have a special place where the Almighty could come to receive the offering in the proper atmosphere. It had to be a place which was Omnipotent. Thus, even the earliest altars, as crude as they appear to be to us, were works of art in their time and made with loving care by those primitive peoples.

"Early altars were made of earth or clay; sometimes stone was added, others were made entirely of stone. The law of Moses permitted altars of either clay and earth or of stone.

"Ordinarily, exponents of this form of worship state, the altar may be any place in the home which is secluded, a place where, when one is meditating or at prayer, there is less likelihood of constant interruption.

"Set aside a place in the home that is quiet, where there will be no interruptions when in meditation and prayer. The attic, the basement, play room, the bedroom, a spare room; all are suitable for the purpose. It is not necessary to have a specially built altar, as any space dedicated to this purpose serves as the altar when the candles are properly arranged.

"Such an arrangement consists of a rectangular area such as a bureau top or a space of equal size. Two candle sticks are placed at the two back corners of this space and in them are inserted two white candles. Personally, I prefer using white candles moulded in the shape of a crucifix. They have their own base, and require no Candlestick holders ... and they are beautiful!

"An Altar Cloth may be spread over the area thus described, if desired.

"This then comprises the altar."

"You Shall Build There An Altar"

DEFINITION OF ALTAR

Having looked into the history of hoodoo altars, let us step back and consider what, exactly, an altar is, and what sets it apart from a kitchen table. An altar is a focal point for a religious or spiritual ritual. It is a raised place that is considered God's table. The origins of the word altar mean "high" and "to ritually burn or sacrifice." In the most basic sense, an altar is a place where spiritual work is going on. An intersection or crossroads between the spirit world and this world, the altar is a place where many types of spiritual practice may be conducted, from meditation to spell-casting. Altars function as a way to distinguish mundane space from the special space where conjure is crafted. "Altar work" is a term rootworkers often use for a spiritual rite or magical spell that we perform at an altar.

Altars come in many types, from the ornate and adorned altars in magnificent cathedrals to humble home altars set out upon a small table or a nightstand. Keeping altars is not necessary for a strong and authentic hoodoo practice. However, many rootworkers maintain an altar at which to create spells, worship and pray, hold candle services, and conduct spiritual rites. Even home practitioners who serve only themselves, their families, and their neighbours are likely to have some sort of altar in their homes.

Early accounts of hoodoo speak of African-style altars on the floor; this is the type described by Helen Pitkin. Floor altars are still found in some African-derived traditions, such as Voodoo, but by the early 1900s, as Black Americans acquired homes and candle magic increased in popularity, raised altars on furniture became the norm in conjure practice.

Home altars are sometimes basic activity areas, where tricks can be put together. When no spells are underway, these areas may be used as mundane surfaces: a place for eating, the surface of a wood-burning stove.

Home altars may kept in secret places, like a closet, or on shared spaces with more than one purpose, such as a mantelpiece, bookcase, or vanity table. A dresser with a pair of taper candles, a Bible, and a photo of an absent family member on top might not even register as an altar for most people, but someone in the know would easily be able to discern that the owner of said dresser decorated it with spiritual intent and purpose.

Often home altars are deliberately hidden in plain sight or made to look like something else entirely. The reason for this is not so much to hide one's spirituality from a disapproving world as it is to keep hidden one's attempts to rule and control those in close proximity. Family members who throw roots often want to keep their spell-casting under wraps because you can't lay sneaky tricks when all the evidence is present and visible in the kitchen. Nothing stands out more than a large altar table covered with candles, herbs, and Magnetic Sand when the in-laws come over. If you want to keep your work a secret, a complex altar is not practical.

Professional hoodoo practitioners tend to be more open about their altars. Throwing tricks or casting spiritual spells for clients generally requires a dedicated, sacred space. The altars of conjure professionals who do not serve as spiritual ministers are primarily their work areas — places where spells are created and put together on the behalf of clients.

Root doctors not only offer their services as readers and spell-casters; it isn't unusual for one to also be a midwife, hairdresser, or herbalist. In this dual capacity they may have altars in both of their professional spaces. Those who take on clients may make their altars accessible to the public. It is at these community altars that root doctors offer prescriptions to their clients.

Candle store and herb shop owners may also maintain display or "demonstration" altars in their stores for the education of customers and for community prayers or justice spells. People will often travel great distances to have jobs done on their behalf at one of these altars.

If a candle worker or shop keeper is also a church deacon, reverend, apostle, minister, or bishop, his or her altar practices on behalf of clients may be called a candle ministry. A rootworker who maintains a candle ministry is likely to have at least one altar set aside as sanctified space where candles are lit or lights are set on behalf of clients. Many candle workers maintain multiple separate candle altars for different client conditions and situations.

To sum up, hoodoo altars may be constructed for spell casting, for reverence and veneration, for spiritual connections, for prayer, as a work surface, or as a place to burn candles. They come in a variety of sizes, shapes, and forms. They may be secret, hidden in plain sight, shown only to clients, or open to the public. They may be created for a wide range of conditions, and those conditions may be mixed and matched with other conditions on the same surface, as space may allow.

In hoodoo there isn't only one right reason or way to build an altar.

BASIC TYPES OF ALTARS

When you break it down to the most simple definition, there are really only two types of altars: working altars and shrines. There is some amount of cross-over or overlap between them. You may find that your working altar becomes a shrine or your shrine becomes a working altar, but understanding the difference between the two is important at the outset.

GENERAL PURPOSE WORKING ALTARS
A working altar is a dedicated area where you pray and cast spells. It is where the magic is initiated. It can be erected as a temporary surface on which to perform a specific job, used once, and then dismantled, or it can be built as a permanent place for ongoing rootwork, kept clean, and used again and again. Whether you are a home practitioner or a professional conjurer, your working altar will be where you spend most of your time.

It is a good idea to keep your working altar clean. Don't let it get overly cluttered or messy. Take care of the space by cleaning up after spell-casting as well as by regular dusting, washdowns, or suffumigations to keep it fresh. Additionally, you may want to give it an annual spiritual cleansing.

My personal working altar is a large roll-top desk that I have in a dedicated space in my living room. The desk has lots of drawers, pockets, and cubbies where I keep all of my herbs, oils, sachet powders, incense, bath crystals, petition papers, lighters, candles, snuffers, matches, stones, bottles, jars, and so on. On the desktop I have candles burning and honey jars working for clients. This is also where I fix up mojo hands, perform moving candle spells, and work with skull candles for clients. At any one point I may have over two dozen spells going on. This is a working altar that is not dedicated to one condition or spell. If I were to snuff out the lights, I could roll the top down and visitors would not notice that it is an altar.

WORKING CANDLE ALTARS
Rootworkers utilize candle altars as dedicated spaces where they set lights for their clients. What distinguishes working candle altars from other working altars is that they are always constructed as fire-safe areas. If a spiritual practitioner agrees to set lights for you on a candle altar, you may be asked to provide a petition paper or photo to be placed under the candle or to purchase a candle dressed and blessed for your intentions and needs.

WORKING ALTARS FOR SPECIFIC CONDITIONS

All of your rootwork can happen on one altar without trouble or issues, but depending on how your home, church, or shop is laid out, you may be able to dedicate separate altars to specific types of spells.

For example, you might have one altar for love, another for money, a third for protection, and a fourth for social justice cases. These are sometimes referred to as condition altars because they are used when addressing specific needs, desires, or conditions. If you have one large working altar and the condition altars are smaller, they may also be called side-altars.

If you are a home practitioner who uses conjure regularly, you may find it convenient to have several dedicated altars for different conditions. When the altars are not in active use, you can disassemble and put them away, or you can leave them up as shrines or a places of veneration.

Some professionals dedicate individual altars for every single condition they address on behalf of clients. These may include love altars, harmony or peace altars, money and luck altars, altars for health and healing, uncrossing and jinx breaking altars, protection altars, and cursing altars.

Rootworkers who perform enemy work or cast crossing spells or curses on behalf of clients often do their general spiritual jobs at one altar, except for curses. They then make a side-altar, away from the working altar, for destructive spells alone. It is common for a Southern-style conjure doctor to place such work in the bathroom, under, near, or on top of the toilet tank.

RELIGIOUS AND SPIRITUAL ALTARS

People who venerate and petition ancestors, the dead, spirit guides, or Catholic saints may construct specialized altars in order to honour these entities. How a person creates and maintains a religious altar is a matter of family custom, training, or individual belief.

A number of religious altars were described in the previous chapter on historical hoodoo altars. The careful reader will note that a feature of some, but not all, of those altars was a prayer bench or "kneeler" which was provided for the use of supplicants. Other workers seemed to expect that their clients would simply kneel on the floor.

Among those who belong to certain initiatic religions, there are often proper and improper ways to build and furnish altars, so please be aware that what you read in this book may not apply to altars associated with a religion such as Wicca, Santeria, Palo, or Vodou.

SHRINES: ALTARS OF VENERATION

A shrine is an altar of veneration, an altar that exists for the honour or worship of one or more spirits. Among these are ancestor altars, family altars, memorials to the dead, or religious altars, such as one dedicated to God, a saint or saints, or other holy spirits. Shrines are altars where you can sit in prayer or meditation, make offerings, and honour the spirits with whom you are working or who you desire to contact.

Altars for ancestor veneration or the memorialization of the dead are frequently kept separate from other spell-work. These altars can be as simple as a place with a picture of an ancestor with a single candle, or as elaborate and intricate as a permanent installation with flowers, mementos, and regular offerings of food and drink.

In hoodoo we find many formal and informal veneration altars for those who lived on Earth and have died, especially those who were also revered in life. Jesus is certainly the most often encountered of these, and his statues — both as a Black man and as a White man — are found in many homes. Not on the same level of spirituality, but also revered, is Black Hawk, a Native American Sauk and Fox Tribe warrior who came into hoodoo via the Spiritual Church Movement and its founder, Mother Leafy Anderson. Spiritualist Church mediums frequently seek contact with Native American spirit guides, and Anderson honoured Black Hawk in this way. After her death, his veneration spread throughout Black Spiritualist circles.

Social and spiritual leaders like Martin Luther King Jr., John F. Kennedy, Harriet Tubman, Sojourner Truth, Marie Laveau, and Bob Marley are also found on home shrines, where they may be represented by a framed picture or a statue. Catholics, of course, have their saints, among whom is Saint Martin de Porres, the first Black man to be canonized by the Catholic Church and a prominent figure in hoodoo.

In Thai and Chinese restaurants you may see shrines for Buddha, Nan Kwak, General Kung, or Maneki Neko the Beckoning Cat, where business owners, employees, and customers leave offerings. Due to the Asian influence on West Coast hoodoo, there are also home shrines created for Hotei, called Hotei-Buddha, the potbellied Chinese deity of good fortune.

Similar to shrines of veneration are shrines of hope, in which the person being venerated is still alive, and so these altars are considered to support the living. Images of President Barack Obama, for instance, are found on shrines of honour created by those who support him.

ALTAR WORK OR JUST PLAIN WORK?

A common question that people ask about altars in the tradition of conjure is: "Is the rootwork that I am doing just rootwork or is it altar work?" What this question really boils down to is: "Do I need to have an altar?"

The simple answer is no, you can practice hoodoo and never once create or use an altar. It isn't a requirement. And yet, here we have an entire book dedicated to hoodoo altars, and we know that they have a long history, so obviously they have some value, right?

You can perform rootwork without having a dedicated altar space, but whether you realize it or not, if you are practicing conjure, the space that you are working on *is* an altar, even if you aren't dedicating it to be a regular working space. These two seemingly different concepts do go hand-in-hand — but although a special altar room or an elaborate altar with red velvet fringe isn't required in order to practice hoodoo, many spiritual spell-casters do prefer to create these sacred spaces in order to more fully develop the connection with the spirits they contact.

Why do people want to go to the trouble of making altars with fabric coverings, Bibles, candles and candle stands, incense burners, pictures, and statuary — not to mention oils, herbs, washes — just to do down-home style conjuring that you could do on your kitchen table? Well, by contrast, your kitchen table, while perfectly adequate for staging a quick candle spell or crafting a mojo hand, would be an unlikely spot on which to burn a 21-day run of job-getting or love-drawing candles. What distinguishes an altar from a kitchen table, therefore, may be more than appearance — it may also be its convenience.

An altar that is set aside for spiritual practices is also a place of power where you can intensify your focus. Its very creation can be of great help to your conjure work. No matter the spell you want to perform, an altar gives you a point of focus. Standing or kneeling in front of your altar provides a place to shift your awareness and to clearly see your goals.

The reality is that when you make an altar you are making a small sacred space in your home. This is why it is so important for you to take the time to intentionally design the space where you will do the work and to be deliberate and clear with your intention through the entire process. Intention goes a long way and you will see that through this dedication, your spell-casting will become more effective.

ALTARS FOR WHAT PURPOSE?

What are the reasons that hoodoo practitioners have altars? There are as many reasons as there are altars. Professional rootworkers and home practitioners alike have altars dedicated to a diverse set of conditions and purposes. Some practitioners like to split all of the conditions they handle into separate areas, while others, whether out of preference or out of need, just have one main altar for all of their spell-casting and spiritual prayers, no matter what condition they're dealing with.

Any type of spell that you want to do can have an altar built or a space set aside to support the work. Here is a breakdown of some of the more common conditions we can address or remediate with hoodoo, but this is just a launching-point, because the list could go on for several pages:

- **Blessings and Opportunities**
- **Health and Healing**
- **Ancestor Veneration or Memory**
- **Reverence for or Contact with Spirits, Angels, Saints, or God**
- **Love, Romance, Marriage, and Reconciliation**
- **Peace in the Home, Cooperation in the Family**
- **Money Luck and Good Fortune**
- **Job-Getting, Workplace Harmony, and Employment Security**
- **Safe Travel and Return**
- **Court Case or Legal Issues**
- **Physical and Spiritual Protection**
- **Uncrossing, Jinx Breaking, and Curse Lifting**
- **Break Ups and Hot Footing**
- **Cursing and Destruction**

Before you start down the road to creating your altar, the first thing you need to decide is what this altar will be used for. This is the first question that you should be asking yourself, because this answer will help to determine your next steps. What do you want to do? What is the purpose of the rootwork you are planning? Who are the spirits, guides, or ancestors that you want to communicate with? This might seem like a simple question to answer, but you need to have real clarity on what your rootwork is going to look like in order to create the right atmosphere.

BUILDING THE ALTAR

Once you have determined the type of altar that you want to create, cleaned the area, and started to pick out the items that you will be using on your altar, then it is time to put all the pieces together. I think of this process like creating a pizza. You start with the dough, which is the surface that all the other ingredients will rest upon. Then you add the sauce, which equates to your powders or fabrics, and from that point the remaining ingredients are placed on top of the pizza based on your personal preferences and needs.

At this point you could dive right in and set down your altar cloth, your statues, candles, and Bible, but first there is one important step that can lay the foundation for powerful spell-casting. Before placing all of the items on your chosen altar surface, start by aligning the area with the conjure work that you are planning.

For example; if you are setting up a money altar, first dust your altar space with some Money Drawing Sachet Powder. If it is a love altar, use a wash made with Dixie Love Bath Crystals. Making a protection altar? Try suffumigating your altar space with Protection Incense. If you're putting together an altar for the Archangel Michael, use some Archangel Michael Oil in a five-spot pattern on the altar surface. All of these options can also be mixed and matched depending on your personal preferences, so try a few things and see what you like best.

The more steps that you can take during the altar creation process to match the intention of what you are trying to create, the more elegant your rootwork will be. These layers of activity create a strong pattern that helps to support the spells that you create on your altar space. I would encourage you not to rush this process. Take your time with altar creation and be intentional with each layer you add.

PLACEMENT OF ALTARS AND SHRINES

Once you determine what kind of altar you want to build, you need to determine where you will place it. Don't let space, or a lack thereof, inhibit you. There are so many wonderful and creative ways to design the space that you have. And remember, an altar doesn't have to be obvious. It is likely that you already have a couple of places in your home that will be perfect for what you need.

ALTARS ON EXISTING FURNITURE

You don't need special furniture for your altar. It is possible to use what you already have. Look around your space right now; you probably have a piece of furniture in the room with you that would make an excellent altar.

- **Doorway, Threshold, Lintel:** By creating an altar in your doorway you can control the type of people or spirits allowed into your space.
- **Hall Tree:** A great place to put a protection altar, as it is often the first item passed when entering a home and usually faces the front door.
- **Mantelpiece:** The mantel is an easy place to put an altar for home or family harmony, as well as ancestor veneration of a semi-public nature.
- **Bookcase or Entertainment Center:** The top of an entertainment center or bookcase is often unused; it's a quiet place to build an altar.
- **Curio Shelf or Wall Shelf:** Shelves function well for people who have limited space or who want a simple altar that doesn't need a lot of space.
- **Wall or Plate Rail:** It is traditional to arrange photos of ancestors on a wall or along a plate rail; a small table below serves as the altar.
- **Table or Work Bench:** Used coffee tables, kitchen tables, side tables, end tables, and carpenter's work benches can be found at thrift stores.
- **Nightstand:** These are excellent for love spells and for night-time protection because they are right next to your bed.
- **Bureau, Lowboy, Dresser, Chiffarobe:** These pieces of furniture contain drawers, so they provide storage space for conjure supplies.
- **Vanity:** An altar on a vanity, especially a vanity with a triptych mirror, is useful if your primary private space is in your bedroom.
- **Desk:** A good space for an altar to bring success in your career or business. Sneaky tricks can be placed underneath or in a drawer.
- **Kitchen Cabinet:** An upper kitchen cabinet is an excellent place to store hidden materials and ongoing spells that will be added to foods.
- **Bed:** Many traditional love spells feature the bed as a sort of altar. Marriage, sex, and romance spells are best done in the bed.
- **Window Sill:** Decorative sacred items attract little notice when set on window sills; just be careful not to store herbs or oils in sunlight.
- **Closet Shelf:** The upper shelf in a closet is a good place to build an altar that you need to keep hidden or secret.
- **Behind the Commode:** This is the perfect place for cursing or break ups; it is traditionally used as a place to store vinegar jar spells.

OUTDOOR ALTARS AND SHRINES

Have you ever seen a wayside shrine or a memorial in a park? If you have, you know that an altar doesn't have to be inside a building. You also don't have to be the owner of the space where you build an altar. Consider building a simple and inconspicuous altar in an outdoor public place.

- **Front or Back Porch**: Your front porch or yard is a place for the things that you want to draw into your life. Your back porch or yard is a place for something you want to keep in your life.
- **Patio:** A patio can be used for almost any type of altar, especially if it is screened in and safe from the weather. Try outfitting a portable patio buffet table, console cabinet, wooden keg, or wine barrel as an altar.
- **Barbecue Pit:** You may not have a place inside your home to set vigil lights, but a barbecue pit is fire-safe. You can also use it for cursing, to put heat to someone, or to leave a doll baby in a dark, sooty place.
- **Garden**: Build an altar or shrine in your own garden or a community garden. This would be a good place to lay spells for growth. Rock or brick work will stand up to the elements when it is not in use.
- **Trees**: Send forth desires into the world by placing them up among the leaves of trees. Hide things in hollow trees. To stop up an enemy's life force, drill a hole in a tree, stuff their personal concerns in the hole, cut a plug from the same tree, and hammer it into the hole with nine blows.
- **Crossroads:** A crossroads is a place where root doctors may leave spell remains, but it can also be an altar for opening your own roads.
- **Graveyard:** A graveside altar or bench may be used for ancestor veneration, laying floral tributes, or setting lights, but also consider taking problems to a gravesite and burying them there.

ALTARS AS SPECIAL FURNITURE

Creating an altar as its own special piece of furniture need not involve fine carpentry. Back in the days of giant wooden speaker cabinets, it was quite common to repurpose them into full time altars by draping gold lamé cloth over them. Speaker cabinets are verging on antiques now, but having a piece of furniture dedicated for use as an altar will add a unique touch to your home. You can repurpose or custom design an altar to include drawers, shelves, and additions that make it fully-functional and available to store your magical items, as well as providing a surface where you can do your work.

ALTARS ON THE WALL

In many traditions around the world altars are hung on walls. They range from single pieces of art to colourful tapestries. Some take the form of decorative boxes that hold statuary, prayers, and sacred anointed objects.

In every Catholic church you will find a hanging altar. It hangs right behind the main altar table and it holds the church's most sacred symbol: the crucifix. This is also the main focal point of the Catholic altar.

In Mexico there are nichos, small altar boxes dedicated to a specific saint or the Virgin Mary. They often come in bright colours with scalloped or curved edges and a glass front to protect the items inside the altar box.

In hoodoo we sometimes find altars hung in the corner of a room. A wooden corner curio shelf may be such an altar. Hanging a framed picture in the corner is another option. Anyone seeing this altar will think you have just hung up a lovely framed picture, but with the right dressings and blessings, that picture frame you've hung up becomes a fully-functioning altar.

One way to be smart with your space is to purchase a shadow box and create your own wall altar. A shadow box is a simple wooden box with a glass front so you can see what is inside, much like the Mexican nichos. With a shadow box you can create an altar for any purpose you want, hang it anywhere that you would like, or anywhere that it will fit. These boxes are inexpensive and can be arranged in a way that calls to your sense of style. They can also be blessed with smoke or powders and used as a travelling altar when other means of altar creation aren't advisable or possible.

TRIPTYCH ALTARS

A triptych altar is a three-panelled altar. This was a very popular art form in early Christian art and it is commonly found in churches. There is one on the cover of this book.

The middle panel of a triptych is usually the largest, while the two side panels are smaller, generally half the size of the middle panel. The three panels may be flat or they may be made up of shallow open boxes containing figurines or imagery in each box that flow together to create one scene. The two panels on the sides of a triptych altar may be able to fold shut. If they are open boxes with finished backsides, then when the triptych is closed, it is not revealed to be an altar but looks like a wooden storage box.

Many old-fashioned bedroom vanity sets have triptych-style mirrors; this lends them to natural use as altars.

ONE ALTAR OR MANY?

The question of how many altars to make is addressed by Reverend Catherine Yronwode of Missionary Independent Spiritual Church as follows:

MANY SINGLE PURPOSE ALTARS

"Some people make dedicated altars for certain types of spells — money and jobs, love and sex, protection and blessings, coercions and curses. If you do that, you can keep each altar set the way it is on a permanent basis. You might end up with four or more altars, and if you add extra shrines for special spiritual entities or ancestors, you might have a dozen or more."

TWO OPPOSING ALTARS OF INCREASE AND DECREASE

"Another way to set up altars — and limit them to two — is to divide your spells into those of increase and those of decrease. Increase can bless ('bring me love') or curse ('bring him death'), likewise, decrease can bless ('remove poverty') or curse ('remove the neighbours'). If you do that, you can work all spells of increase at an altar that faces East ('As the Sun rises, bring to me xxx') and all spells of decrease at an altar that faces West ('As the Sun sets, remove xxx from me'). The two altars can be on two sides of the same room."

THE LONG ALTAR IN THREE PARTS

"If you only have room for one altar, have it be wider than long and run it along the south wall of your room. Work the east end (the left side as you face South) for increase, and the west side (the right side as you face South) for decrease. The middle (due South, the high noon position of the Sun) is used for all spells of sustaining, protection, and blessing. Deacon Millett of Four Altars Gospel Sanctuary has a granite-topped altar, about 4 feet long, sectioned off like this. I have seen him work a Peaceful Home spell in the center, a Reversing spell on one side and a Money Drawing spell on the other — with each section of the altar as its own separate territory of intentionality."

THE SQUARE OR CIRCULAR ALTAR IN FOUR PARTS

"If you work by the four elements, four seasons, or four directions, divide a square or circular table into four sections, like the Congo cosmogram or hoodoo five-spot pattern. Situate your job in the quadrant that best suits it. Any unused section can hold a marker of its symbolism, such as a statue."

PRACTICAL ALTAR TIPS

If you are new to altar work, here are some things you should know:

FIRE SAFETY
When you work with open flame, do so carefully and safely.
Never leave fire unattended.
Make sure that you only use fire-safe items as candle holders. This prevents them from breaking, melting, or catching on fire as the wax melts.
Check to be certain that the smoke alarms in your home are operating properly and keep the batteries fresh. Also make sure that you have the recommended number of smoke alarms.
Invest in a fire extinguisher just in case there are any emergencies or accidents. And keep it near your candle-burning area.
If there is anything you value and don't want to see burned, covered in wax, or ruined, don't use it or store it where you will be working with fire.

WAX SPILLS
Wax will melt and it has a tendency to get all over everything. Be cautious when you remove wax from your altars. Peeling or chipping wax off of a wooden surface can chip off varnish or paint.
If wax gets on carpet or fabric let it dry first, then cover the area with a paper bag. Use an iron on the coolest setting you can and place that warmed up iron on top of the paper bag. The spilled wax will heat up and transfer from your fabric or carpet onto the bag. This will easily remove that wax from your carpet or fabric without ruining it. Then you can determine if you will just toss that wax out or if you need to ritually dispose of it.

STORAGE SPACE
No matter how often you work at the altar or what kind of work you do, you need tools. You should have a range of bowls, plates, and trays; holders for candles; jars for herbs; and containers for incenses, oils, or powders. If yours is a devotional altar, you will need a way to hold offerings of water, food, drink, perfumes, cigars, coins, or flowers. If you will be burning candles, you will need a set of candle tools. All of these tools require storage space. Plan the storage space into your altar, if you can. The best place is under your altar, using drawers, pull outs, or shelves.

ALTAR PARAPHERNALIA

A wide variety of objects and tools can be found on hoodoo altars. In selecting items to place on your altar, it is wise to both follow traditional cultural patterns and to allow yourself free range in the matter of personal preference and choice.

Depending on the type of furniture on which you are building the altar, how you will be using it, and your own aesthetic viewpoint, your altar may look like an art installation or a spare and austere countertop. By now it should be clear that there isn't one right way to build or decorate an altar and that altars are a great place to express your artistic individuality. Let yourself have fun with it, try a few things, see what get results for you, and be prepared to change your altar around when you feel the call to do so, just as you might redecorate your living room.

The next few pages are devoted to listing the basic types types of altar accessories, objects, and tools, explaining what they are used for, and why you might want to acquire them. You won't need all of this paraphernalia, of course, but do explore the possibilities, while keeping in mind the realities of your living space, your budget, your family and friends, and the conjure work that you are doing. Let these pages be a starting point to help you build and create your own personal altars.

BASIC ALTAR ACCESSORIES

Here are the most common altar accessories used by professional root doctors and home practitioners alike:

- **Candles, Oil Lamps, Candle Stands, and Candle Tools** 30
- **Incense and Incense Burners** 32
- **Floral Offerings, Living Plants, or Silk Flowers** 33
- **Jars, Glasses, Bowls, Plates, Trays, Mortars, and Pestles** 34
- **Writing Supplies for Name, Petition, and Prayer Papers** 34
- **Statuary, Prints, Pictures, and Photographs** 35
- **Herbs, Roots, Curios, and Craft Supplies** 36
- **Altar Cloths** 36
- **The Bible** 38
- **Reference Books** 38

ALTAR CANDLES AND LAMPS

If you will be praying with or performing spells with candles, order ahead. Being prepared with a variety of candles — and a variety of candle holders — will save you from last minute emergencies. Keep a lamp on hand, too, in case you can't get candles in on time. Holders, stands, and candelabras can easily be found in any local thrift shop or second-hand store. Star holders, the most inexpensive stands, are purchased from occult shops.

Here are some common types of candles:

- **Pillar Candles:** These are solid and stand on their own, but they do have a tendency to melt all over the place. Candle holders can prevent that, as can setting pillar candles in a bowl or deep-sided dish.
- **Taper or Dinner Candles:** These are long, thin candles used in candelabras. They require well-fitting candle stands, as they can easily tip over and drip wax.
- **Offertory or Household Candles:** There are six-inch straight-sided candles; they require stands. Star holders come in two sizes, and the larger size is a cheap holder for them.
- **Jumbo and Double-Action Candles:** These are nine-inch straight-sided candles; they require stands. Plain jumbos are burned from top to bottom; two-tone double-action candles are burned upside down.
- **Chime Candles or Altar Lights:** These are the four-inch candles used for sweer jars, for spells with multiple candles, and for times when you want a quick-burning light. The small star holders are made to fit them.
- **Votive and Tea Lights:** These are small candles that are usually burned in containers of glass, stone, or metal. When votives are burned without a container, some folks call them "stubbies."
- **Figural Candles:** These are molded hard wax candles available in a variety of shapes, including men, women, couples, 7-knobs, skulls, genitals, devils, hearts, animals, hands, and more.
- **Glass-Encased Candles or Vigil Lights:** These are eight-inch tall glass tubes filled with soft, gooey wax. They typically burn for several days. They are considered safer to burn than free-standing candles.
- **Kerosene and Vegetable Oil Lamps:** These are employed in long-term spells; the lamp reservoirs can be used to hold magical curios. Kerosene or mineral lamp oil burns bright; vegetable oil is cleaner.

ASSEMBLING A SET OF CANDLE MAGIC TOOLS
The following is a list of candle magic tools reprinted from *The Art of Hoodoo Candle Magic* by Catherine Yronwode and Mikhail Strabo:

- A flat, level, fireproof surface made of stone, metal, or tile.
- Metal containers such as buckets, steam-table trays, and/or bread pans.
- Saucers and bowls of brass, oven-proof glass, and white chinaware.
- A cookie sheet plus optional aluminum foil for rolling candles.
- Fireproof holders, burners, braziers, and/or ash catchers for incense.
- Clean sand to line buckets, bowls, trays, pans, and incense pots.
- A stove or hot plate and a small pan or large spoon in which to melt wax.
- Hollow candle stands to conceal spells, metal lug-jar lids for insulation.
- Stamped metal star holders and a menorah for setting multiple candles.
- A metal candle snuffer; it can also be used as a cone-shaper for incense.
- Paper, pencils, pens, and inks for writing out petitions and prayers.
- One or more books of Solomonic or Mosaic seals, if you work with them.
- Scissors and pinking shears to trim wicks and cut out papers and seals.
- A glue stick for affixing copies of photos, seals, or art to vigil candles.
- Inscribing and carving tools: needle, nail, awl, screwdriver, or pen-knife.
- Pins and needles for sectional marking and for piercing candles.
- Kitchen tongs or a long surgical hemostat for "saving" drowning lights.
- Wooden matches, both household and fireplace size.
- Bamboo skewers for transferring flame from one candle to another.
- Tapers or lighter-candles if you dislike the use of matches or skewers.
- Saved wick-trimmings from vigil candles to use as splint-wicks.
- A mirror tile (a 3"-4" circle or square is sufficient) for Reversing spells.
- Glass photo-coasters to use as covers for seals, photos, sigils, or petitions.
- Anointing oils to dress lights for a variety of spiritual conditions.
- Herbs, roots, and minerals for dressing, rolling, and/or loading candles.
- Incense, including hoodoo herbal powder incense, resins, agarbatti joss sticks, dhoop cones, and briquette incense; plus charcoal disks.
- Sachet powders for "double dressing" oiled candles and for drawing patterns such as triangles, stars, or crosses on the altar.
- Clean-up materials for wax and soot on altars, walls, and ceilings.
- A small wall-mounted home fire extinguisher.
- A Bible or Book of Psalms. The entire Book of Psalms is online here: **ReadersAndRootworkers.org/wiki/Category:The Book of Psalms**

INCENSE ON THE ALTAR

Many spells call for incense; after all, the Bible says to burn incense! At your working altar you will want to have a place where you can safely burn incenses of many types and styles.

In hoodoo practice, incense is not only utilized as an inspiring source of fragrance; it is used to smoke objects or items such as mojo hands or doll babies as they are being crafted. There are plenty of condition incenses, like Come To Me, Crown of Success, Fast Luck, and so on, that you can burn to help with your conjure work, but there are other choices with incense too.

Pay attention to the type of incense that you select because it may require a specialized burner. Additionally, be aware that some kinds of incense are not available in specific scents. Try out a few types of incense and see which kind your prefer. Make sure that you burn something that you actually enjoy.

FORMS OF INCENSE
- **Stick Incense or Agharbatti:** This is incense powder that has been affixed, often with a resin, to a wooden stick for burning.
- **Charcoal Disk:** An unscented charcoal that burns like a barbecue briquette; once it is lit, incense powders and herbs are burned on it.
- **Incense Powders:** Powders come in two types, self-lighting, which burn on their own, and non-self-lighting, which must be set on charcoal.
- **Condition Incense**: A blend of incense powder and herbs created for specific spell needs, usually in the form of self-lighting incense powders.
- **Briquette Incense:** This is a scented charcoal square or rectangle; when it is lit, it gives off a fragrance.
- **Coil Incense**: Similar to stick incense, it is in a coil shape with no central stick; it is hung up, uncoiled, and lit from the bottom.
- **Loose Herbs**: Herbs can be burned as incense but they will need a heat source to keep going; a charcoal disk is most commonly used.
- **Resin Incense:** Hardened tree saps or resins that give off a fragrance as they burn are crumbled and set on charcoal disks.
- **Dhoop Sticks or Logs:** Similar to coil incense or to stick incense without the stick, dhoop logs are formed into cylinders.
- **Cone Incense:** A type of dhoop incense that is formed into a cone shape and can be burned without a heat source.

INCENSE BRAZIERS AND BURNERS
Here are the most common types of containers for incense:

- **Ash Catcher:** Long and flat, ash catchers are used to burn stick incense. You can find ash catchers made from wood, resin, clay, metal, glass, ceramics, and stone. Be careful: the wooden ones can catch on fire!
- **Bowl Burner:** Metal bowls can safely hold burning incense. If you wish to put a piece of charcoal in the bottom to burn herbs or powder incenses, the bowl should be lined with clean sand.
- **Brazier:** This is a metal pan or stand that can be used for hot coals; lined with clean sand, it is a holder for charcoal disks and and any incense you wish to burn on them. Many braziers are three-legged.
- **Cauldron:** This is a rounded cast-iron cooking pot; its shape has been replicated in miniature for use as an incense burner. Cauldrons are strong, sturdy and fire-safe; the three-legged ones disperse heat best.
- **Censer:** Made of brass and other metals, a censer is similar to a thurible, but without the chain. They often have pierced covers or sides. They should be lined with sand to protect the container.
- **Coil Burner:** This is a specialized holder or hook from which one can hang acoil of incense; the coil is then lit from the bottom. Coil incense won't burn if it is lying on a flat surface.
- **Combination Burner:** These are burners made to accommodate a variety of different types of incense, such as stick and cone. They come in a diverse array of styles.
- **Cone Burner:** Cone incense is a self-lighting incense and will burn completely, so any fire-safe surface will do, but cone burners are generally made in the form of decorative stone, metal, or ceramic disks.
- **Thurible:** This is a metal censer suspended from chains. Thuribles are swung side-to-side during religious services to spread the aroma of the incense. They are lined with sand to protect the metal from burn-out.

FLORAL OFFERINGS, PLANTS, SILK FLOWERS

Hearkening back to a time when it was the custom to provide evidence of Nature's bounty on the altar, flowers, plants, harvested fruits, festive boughs, and, if all else fails, artistic silk flowers are not only offerings; they remind us of the world in which we exist and live our lives of hope and struggle.

JARS, GLASSES, BOWLS, PLATES, AND TRAYS

Both shrines of veneration and working altars are usually supplied with an assortment of containers that are strong, sturdy, and easy to clean. You will use them to hold incense, burn or store candles, present offerings, grind up ingredients, store herbs, hide burned matchsticks, roll candles, and so on.

- **Jars:** Storage jars are generally considered to be utilitarian, but if they are decorative, they may sit out on the altar while work is being done. They may also be placed out of sight when not in use.
- **Glasses:** Water goblets and glasses are used to hold liquid offerings on the altar. The use of water to draw spirits is common in folk magic; in Spiritist practices, a crucifix may be placed in a water goblet as well.
- **Bowls:** In addition to their use as tools for mixing up herbs, incenses, powders, or oils, bowls can do double duty as candle holders if you pour sand, dirt, sugar, or salt into their bottom and stand candles in them.
- **Plates and Saucers:** Thick white restaurant-ware plates and saucers find traditional uses on altars in Spiritual Churches where they are turned over and used to cover petitions and other items being worked on.
- **Trays:** Metal trays are used when rolling candles in herbs and also for moving candle spells and Lodestone spells, to contain the work. When lined with sand, they provide a temporary fire-proof surface.
- **Mortars and Pestles:** You will need at least two sets of these tools, one fine (porcelain, marble, wood, brass, or soapstone) and one coarse (lava rock, granite, or cast iron) to reduce herbs and roots to powder.

WRITING SUPPLIES

Although not entirely necessary at shrines of veneration, writing supplies, including papers of various types and weights, pencils, pens, markers, and inks, are essential for those who maintain working altars. Glue, stickers, envelopes, and other stationery supplies are useful as well.

Not to be seen on the altar itself, but certainly desirable in supporting roles, are a computer, a colour printer, a graphics program such as Photoshop, and a small library of type fonts.

For in-depth lessons on name papers, petitions, and prayer papers, see:
"Paper in My Shoe" by Catherine Yronwode

STATUARY

If you are building an altar or shine to a spirit, saint, or deity, statuary is a great way to dedicate your space and align it with the specific spirit.

In some spiritual lineages the statue is an extension of the spirit it is made to represent. It may be empowered in such a way that the spirit inhabits it. When you use a statue like that you are inviting the energy of that spirit into your home and your altar.

Statues may also serve as markers of those who now live on in spirit form. For example, among Christian Spiritualists, the spirit of Black Hawk is represented by a Black Hawk bucket. This is a metal farm bucket filled with sand or dirt, on top of which sets a figure of a Native American, with arrows, spears, and/or the American flag. Black Hawk is a protector, so these shrines are placed near doors or entranceways, where Black Hawk serves as a watcher on the wall. He may be given offerings of water, fruit, Corn, or Tobacco.

When you have statues on your altar it is important to keep them clean and cared for to show respect to the entity that statue is connected to.

PICTURES, PRINTS, AND WALL ART

Having beautiful items around and above your altar space will make it a place where you want to spend time.

Images of the people for (or against) whom you are working are essential as personal concerns. If you are casting love spells to bring a former lover back to you, you will want a picture of your target on your altar space.

If you are creating a shrine for a spirit, or asking a spirit's help, you may want to have a print or tapestry to gaze upon. Figures from the Bible, and the blessed dead of revered memory, will help you focus on spirituality.

Above my prosperity altar there is a beautiful print of Lakshmi, the Hindu goddess of abundance. She reminds me of financial wealth and her spiritual influence aids the money drawing work I do.

Above my working altar there are images of psychics and fortune tellers. These art pieces put me in the right frame of mind for readings and rootwork.

Other friends of mine have pictures of Black Jesus, their ancestors, the Hindu god Shiva, the Temperance card of the Rider-Waite-Smith tarot, the Archangel Michael, or powerful departed humans such as Marie Laveau, Harriet Tubman, Martin Luther King, and Bayard Rustin on their altars.

HERBS, ROOTS, CURIOS, AND CRAFT SUPPLIES

If you make mojo hands or tobies at your working altar, you will need storage space for your roots, herbs, minerals, and curios, plus cloth or leather to make the bags. Scissors, pins, needles, and other sewing supplies are also used directly in the performance of candle magic and other altar work. They will be in sight while in use, so spend the few dollars for a pair of all-steel scissors and donate those orange plastic-handled ones to charity.

ALTAR CLOTHS

An altar cloth is not a necessity, but it has a value beyond mere decoration. Aligned visually with your purpose or desire, it will aid your concentration, and not only will it protect your altar surface, it will provide a convenient way to hide flat items, such as packets or name papers.

Your aesthetic preferences, practical needs, and the type of spells you cast will factor into your selection of altar cloths. Above all, be practical: Using your grandma's antique doily under red figural candles in a moving candle spell is not a good idea, unless you want to ruin it forever or dye it pink.

Here are some styles and types of altar cloths you might consider:

- **Handkerchief or Bandana:** Perhaps the simplest and most utilitarian altar cloths one can use are common handkerchiefs or bandanas in suitable colours for the altars being created. These fuction particularly well for travelling, as well as on temporary altars that are built on the fly.
- **Money Altar Cloth:** Green or gold altar cloths are for drawing in money and wealth, and silver will also do in a pinch. Cloth figured with dollar signs, coins, currency, or lucky emblems can also be a good choice for a money altar. Cloth printed with images of dice, cards, and gambling tools symbolize lucky money. A luxurious fabric that incorporates gold metallic threads is suitable for a wealth altar.
- **Love Altar Cloth:** Red is a colour that develops passion, while pink brings in romance and reconciliation. Patterns of hearts and flowers promote love, as do wedding bells or paired doves. If you are bewitching or compelling someone to love you, a purple cloth symbolizes power. For healing love, a light blue cloth may help. Lavender is a symbolic colour of gay love. White signifies new love or a marriage.

- **Protection Altar Cloth:** White is the most common colour for protection. If the cloth has shiny spangles, mirrors, or silver disks on it, it is said to repel the evil eye. If it is embroidered with a pattern of crosses, it is deemed effective in warding off evil spirits. When performing a Fiery Wall of Protection spell, some people prefer a flame-printed or orange cloth. To keep protection work secret or hidden from outside influences, a black cloth provides a cloak of darkness.
- **Healing Altar Cloth:** A pale blue cloth is useful for healing, but white is far more traditional. A cotton or linen cloth aligns well with healing prayers, as there are what some of the earliest bandages were made from. Re-used hospital linens can also become make-shift altar cloths for health and healing, if you are doing conjure work for someone who is in a hospital or getting surgery.
- **Cursing Altar Cloth:** If you are bringing down an enemy, use a black or a black-and-red altar cloth. Black is best for damage or destruction, while red can create inflammatory reactions. A black bandana printed all over with red chili peppers makes a good altar cloth for hot footing. Cursing altars are often temporary, so using a cloth comes in handy when wrapping up the remains for easy disposal.
- **Court Case Altar Cloth:** When influencing legal matters, use a cloth that is brown. However, if you are keeping the law off of your back or away from your home or workplace, use a blue or silver altar cloth.
- **Success Altar Cloth:** On a success altar, whether it is for success in money, school, business, or test-taking, the colours that you want to use are gold, yellow, purple, or a cloth covered in crowns.
- **Devotional Altar Cloth:** When creating an altar for a specific saint, angel, archangel, deity, or other spirit, take time to research the colours and correspondences that are specifically aligned with that spirit. Doing some basic study will give you these answers. Choose colours that have traditionally appealed to the spirit that you are calling upon.
- **Ancestral Altar Cloth:** Ancestor altars can use a cloth of virtually any colour or style, as long as the cloth or colour is connected to your forebears. A flag from your family's country of origin, colours from your lineage, table linens that belonged to past generations of your family, doilies crocheted by your grandmother, or a special altar cloth pieced from garments that they wore would be the most appropriate. Cover antique cloths with a sheet of tempered glass to preserve them.

THE BIBLE

The predominant religion of Black rootworkers is Christianity, so conjure doctors use the Bible in both prayer and spell-casting. It is also the basis for a form of divination called Bibliomancy in which you open the Bible to a random page and read the message that God has for you.

Having a Bible on the altar or setting your Bible open to specific pages of scripture is a powerful way to infuse words of power into your spells and support the type of rootwork that you are doing. The book itself is also a talisman, a powerful protector against evil.

THE GREAT CONJURE BOOK

"The Bible: All hold that the Bible is the great conjure book in the world. Moses is honoured as the greatest conjurer. The names he knowed to call God by was what give him the power to conquer Pharaoh and divide the Red Sea."
— Zora Neale Hurston, "Mules and Men"

BIBLE UNDER THE BED

In 1937, Harry Hyatt was told, "You put a Bible underneath you — open it to any chapter and turn it down under your pillow. Then you put a pair of open scissors on top and that will keep the hag away."
— Informant #559, Jacksonville, Fla. (695:4) page 147.

REFERENCE BOOKS

If you are new to hoodoo candle spells, these books will help:
"The Guiding Light to Power and Success" by Mikhail Strabo
"The Master Book of Candle Burning" by Henri Gamache
"The Art of Hoodoo Candle Magic" by C. Yronwode and M. Strabo
"The Magic Candle" by Charmaine Dey
"Candle Burning Magic: Rituals for Good and Evil" by Anna Riva
For a complete book on the Bible and scriptural magic in conjure, see:
"Hoodoo Bible Magic" by Miss Michaele and Prof. C. D. Porterfield
For dozens of candle altar spells featuring the Bible, see
"The Master Book of Candle Burning" by Henri Gamache
The entire Book of Psalms is online here:
ReadersAndRootworkers.org/wiki/Category:The Book Of Psalms

MAGICAL AND SPIRITUAL CORRESPONDENCES

Symbolic associations between numbers, colours, times, seasons, and intentions are found in most forms of folk magic. However, because cultures adopted ideas such as formal numeration and calendar-making at different times, there is no universal rule governing correct correspondences. Hoodoo, as an American practice, has drawn from many sources, and although few conjure doctors use all of the possible associations, many will tell you that aligning your altar layout with natural forces does strengthen the work.

For example, if you are doing love work, create your altar on a Friday during a waxing moon in Taurus or Libra, use two candles, and decorate with coral pink and red. These things are in alignment with love.

This isn't a requirement, and rootwork can be just as effective if you can't wait for the full moon two weeks away. However, having things in alignment and using known correspondences will ease your way, add power to your spells, and potentially give your confidence a boost as well.

Here are the most common symbolic correspondences used in spells:

- **Numbers**.. 39
- **Colours**.. 40
- **Days of the Week** 42
- **Moon Phases**... 42

NUMBERS

Numerology can be used to determine the day of the week or the month of the year you create your altar, and also the number of items, such as candles, that are placed on the altar surface.

1: A single purpose, new beginnings, looking internally, promise
2: Partnership, relationships, balance, choices
3: Fulfillment, growth, development, creativity
4: Structure, stability, limitation, material things
5: Challenge, crisis, transformation, change, embodiment
6: Harmony, balance, union, connection, beauty
7: Initiation, luck, mystery, knowledge, analysis
8: Abundance, harvest, manifestation, labour
9: Completion, leadership, power, high standards

COLOURS

Pick items for your altar in the colours that support the work that you will be doing. If you don't have some of the colours, you can always use white, as it is a universal colour for blessing and spirituality.

Colours each have their own vibrational level, and employing them in your altar decor will help to create that vibration for the spiritual task you are undertaking. Just think about certain clothing items that you have and how you feel when you put them on. If the colour of an outfit can help to shift the way that you feel in your ordinary activities, imagine what that colour will do in its symbolic role as part of your spells.

Here are some basic colour associations to help you get started:

- **Red:** Red adds "heat" to any type of spell. This heating can be positive or negative depending on what you want to achieve. The colour red adds hot passion to a love relationship. On the other hand, red contributes hot anger to cursing or hot foot work. This colour can be used to build passion and love or tear down and curse. Choose carefully and be specific in your intention.
- **Orange:** If you are looking to clear away obstacles, open roads, offer protection, or create change, orange is the colour to use, as these are some of the purposes to which orange is connected. Orange can add strength; like the colour red does, but it does this in a way that offers protection and clears away blockages, while offering encouragement.
- **Yellow:** As a softer version of the colour gold, yellow is associated with success and achievement, as well as to the golden coins of money for building income and wealth. This is the colour of the Sun and the positive energy that comes from sunshine, including happiness, joy, and growth. Yellow is also the colour of the will and mastery.
- **Green:** In modern times, green has become connected with money and wealth spells due to the colour of American paper currency. However, green is also the colour of plants, and therefore implies a farmer's harvest of abundance and achievement. As such, it is the colour of fertility and is used for luck, wealth, and financial stability.
- **Blue:** The colour blue is tied to health and healing in many cultures in the world. This symbolic connection may derive from the healing nature of water and of clear skies. Blue is also the colour of psychic development, intuition, dreams, and tranquility.

- **Purple:** Purple is the colour of strength and power and the colour of royalty. This colour offers rulership, dignity, and some amount of control in any of spells you undertake. Purple, like its chromatic neighbour blue, is also a colour that connects to psychic vision, intuition, and spiritual development.
- **Pink:** Gentle shades of pink are connected to romantic love. Pink is a softer version of red, so it offers the love connection without the heat of the passion that red can bring.
- **Brown:** Brown is used in court case and legal work. It is an earth and wood tone, connected to soil and woody plants. It is also associated with animal pelts, many of whose fur is brown in colour. Likewise, the more humble of the Catholic Franciscan saints are identified with brown, the colour of their robes.
- **Black:** The colour of night, black is used extensively for cursing, crossing, jinxing, destruction, and break up spells. However, black isn't only limited to use as a cursing colour, for it can also be used to keep your work hidden, to cover up what you don't want others to see, and to bind negativity. To some it also signifies a memorial to the dead.
- **White:** White represents purity, and it is employed in blessing and protection. It is the colour of peace and holiness. It sanctifies marriages, and it aids in justice work by bringing out the truth. Because of its neutrality, white candles or altar cloths may be used as fill-ins for any other colour, should you have need of a substitute.
- **Silver:** Used in connection with "small-change" money tricks, silver is the colour of many coins. Most currency was originally made from silver, and although this isn't the case with modern money, the connection to silver is still there. Silver can also be used in reversal workings to send evil back to the one who sent it, in the same way a silvered mirror would be used.
- **Gold:** Connected to "high-stakes" money, gold is one of the most valuable metals on the planet. Crowns and fine jewelry are made from gold, so it is also connected to Crown of Success or other spells that bring success. Gold is also a good colour to use when petitionaing saints who are not known to favour certain colours, as it creates happiness and joy.

For more on the use of colour correspondences in candle spells, see **"The Art of Hoodoo Candle Magic" by C. Yronwode and M. Strabo**

DAYS OF THE WEEK
This system of correspondences dates back to the Classical era:

- **Monday:** The energy of the Moon is the best day for femininity. This is a good day for family work, dreams, prayers, and psychic development.
- **Tuesday:** Aligned with the planet Mars, this is a day to bring about fighting, war, and break ups. It is also a day of courage and power.
- **Wednesday:** Connected to the planet Mercury, this is the day for communication or improving verbal skills, as well as for gambling luck.
- **Thursday:** Ruled by the planet Jupiter, this is a good day for work related to money and power as well as generosity and philanthropy.
- **Friday:** In connection to the planet Venus, this is the best day for love spells, sex magic, creating beauty, and for seduction.
- **Saturday:** Aligned with the planet Saturn, this is the day for cursing enemies. It is also the day to impose limitations and restrictions on others.
- **Sunday:** The energy of the Sun is the best day for masculine energy. It is a good day for success, healing, health, and gaining fame.

MOON PHASES
The Moon's phases of growth and diminishment set a natural cycle for us that lasts about 28 days, or one lunar month.

- **Waxing Moon:** During its waxing, the Moon is getting bigger in the sky every night. This is a time for spells to increase or attract, and for pulling in money, love, success, and growth.
- **Full Moon:** When the Moon is fully round in the sky it is called a full moon, This is a good time for love, for encouraging things that have grown to stay, and for venerations, dedications, and peace.
- **Waning Moon:** When the Moon is getting smaller in the sky it is called a waning moon. This is a time for sending things away or banishing, as well as decreasing negative energies such as poverty or sickness.
- **New Moon:** When there is no visible Moon in the sky it is called a dark moon. This is a time for cursing, calling up dark spirits, or trapping and binding negativity.
- **Change of the Moon:** At sunset, generally four nights after the dark moon, when the first sliver of the Moon is seen, it is called the Change of the Moon, a time for bathing and cleansing, and for fresh starts.

CLEANING AND MAINTAINING ALTARS

Just as we would clean a house before moving into it, so do we clean our altars before first using them. Preparatory cleansing should always be your first step in setting up a new altar and, for many, it is also a first step before undertaking any new spells at an existing altar.

It doesn't matter if your new altar will be on a shelf, an end table, an entire room, the backyard, or a temple; altar creation begins with cleaning.

Cleaning can be thought of in two steps. The first step is to clear away any residue that may already be in the space that you will be using. You are neutralizing the area, wiping away anything unintentional or messy.

The second step is analogous to painting on a primer coat before painting a house. You will create a clean space that matches the intent of the conjure work that you will be performing on your altar.

How you carry out the first type of cleaning, the neutralizing part of it, will depend on the physical surface of your altar. This isn't magical, but totally mundane and practical. No matter what cleaning agent you decide to use, you must make sure that it is safe for the surface you are washing.

One of the best cleaners is Chinese Wash, as it is safe on almost all surfaces, and you can also wash altar cloths in it. You might also try an herbal tea mixture that you create as a special wash for your new altar. Making a tea, wash, or scrub water is simple, and many recipes are available. If you have a different favourite cleansing agent, start with that.

If you aren't sure about a product's safety, don't risk it. Be sure that you know it is totally safe before taking action, because you don't want to ruin a lovely piece of furniture by choosing poorly. For example, Florida Water Cologne will take the varnish off a 19th century cabinet, but will not harm one that has a polyurethane-coated finish. If you have a wooden surface, you would not want to use harsh Buffalo Ammonia, which will damage it. If your altar's fireproof surface is a marble stone, you must not wash it down with vinegar or lemon juice, because acidic liquids will literally dissolve it.

If you are worried about making a mistake, consider censing the altar with incense smoke; that will generally be harmless for most surfaces. Censing and whisking are also favoured ways to perform the second stage of cleaning, laying down the first coat of magical intention on the altar.

For more information on making your own baths and washes, read **"Hoodoo Spiritual Baths" by Aura Laforest**

DISPOSAL OF SPELL REMNANTS

Ritual disposal of spell remnants such as wax, ashes, water, or spiritual supplies like oils, perfumes, or powders is similar to the disposal of altar items. Depending on the type of spell you've cast, you could put unused spiritual supplies into storage for later use or wrap everything in the altar cloth and dispose of it all at once. Here are some other traditional choices:

- **Front Yard:** Burying items in your front yard or by your front door draws what you want toward you. It is also a good place to bury protection work to stop unwanted energies from entering your space.
- **Backyard:** To keep the work close to you or your home, you can bury spell remnants in your back yard. This is often done with remnants from marital fidelity spells.
- **Four Corners:** To nail down work you did to keep your property, divide the spell remnants into four packets and bury one at each of the four corners of your lot, spiking it down with a large nail.
- **East or Sunrise:** Disposing of items toward the East or at sunrise opens you up to receive good luck and increase of what you want to bring into your life. This is the more popular way to dispose of bath water.
- **West or Sunset:** Disposing of items to the West or at sunset causes them to leave you, removing illness, closing down negativity, and putting an end to that which is unwanted.
- **Crossroads:** Leaving items at a crossroad is a common way to send a message into the world, disperse or remove unwanted energies, drive people apart, or let go of things you do not want with you.
- **Graveyard:** Disposal at a graveyard brings situations to an end. It can be used for death spells. However, when working with ancestors, you may dispose of items at their graves for safekeeping or as offerings.
- **Laying Tricks:** Certain spells only take effect when the person who is your target steps on or over them. You can mix remnant love powders, for instance, with local dirt to hide the colour, and deploy them on a path.
- **Running Water:** Disposing of remnants into running water will release what you have done and send it away from you. Rivers are often used to send someone away, and get rid of failed love spells.
- **Trees:** Throwing items at a tree is a way to transfer the outcome of the spell to the tree, which can then compost that energy. This is usually done with remnants left over from a cleansing ritual.

- **Sneaky Tricks:** Giving fixed altar items to the target of your spell is an excellent way to work. Think about using a candle holder in a love spell, dressing it with Love Me Oil, and giving it to your target.
- **Donation:** If there are altar items you will no longer use, consider donating them to the local charity shop. Just make sure that you have spiritually cleaned them before sending them off into the world.
- **Recycling:** Many finished altar items or cast off bits of spell work can simply be placed in your weekly recycling bin. For example, all your empty vigil glass containers can be recycled.

Much more information on the disposal of ritual items is online here: **LuckyMojo.com/layingtricks.html by Catherine Yronwode**

ANNUAL CLEANSING AND ALTAR REFRESHMENT

Busy home practitioners and professional spiritual workers have so many altar tasks going on that they can't actually take time to refresh their altars between each job. However, they generally do cleanse their spaces regularly. There are no firm rules on how often or when to do an altar cleansing, but there are some distinct traditional practices. From the standpoint of spiritual cleanliness, if you are going to do a full cleansing of your altar, then you should also clean the home, office, or church in which the altar is located.

One popular method is to undertake a full, thorough, annual cleansing of your altar or working space on the first day of the year. This is something that we do at Missionary Independent Spiritual Church and at the Lucky Mojo Curio Company next door. It is a great way to refresh and renew yourself and to bring new focus to your spiritual practices, especially if you have a large space and can spend an entire day doing nothing but cleaning.

You might feel called to clean your altars once a month, every full moon, or on the solstices and equinoxes. All of those are traditional times as well, and no one will call you wrong for planning things that way.

Alternatively, you might lightly spritz or cense the altar once a month and do a full cleaning once a year. This too is a common practice.

Whenever you decide to clean your altar, make sure that you remove all of the objects, wash the space down with a neutralizing cleaner, and then clean off every single item that goes back on the altar, as well as any tools that you regularly use. If your altar is intricate, take a cell-phone picture to remind yourself how to set everything back up again.

TAKING DOWN AN ALTAR

Although shrines and altars of veneration are generally conceived as permanent, working altars may not be so, at least for home practitioners.

Whether you have just completed a one-time candle spell for a new job or have been setting lights for a difficult family situation for five years, when you have finished the job, it may be time to dismantle the altar. This is true even if the altar furniture itself is a permanent fixture in your home.

Altar take-downs involve more than simple cleaning; you will want to clear away and dispose of items that you don't plan to reuse and, hopefully, you will rebuild the altar for a new purpose. Just as you began your altar with a cleansing, you will now clean the finished altar space, neutralizing the space either to make it a mundane piece of furniture once again or to prepare it so that you can place your next altar on it.

Any permanent altar items that you plan to keep should be given a good and thorough spiritual cleansing, one piece at a time. End by washing down the altar surface or wiping it down with a spiritual cleaner that is appropriate to its physical composition and finish.

If you think that you will want to do the same or a similar spell again, consider cleaning the altar paraphernalia and putting it away in storage for future use. On the other hand, if you are pretty certain that you will never do this type of conjure again, then clean the items and dispose of them in a ritual manner. Give them away, burn them, or bury them.

One option for handling unwanted supplies is to wrap up all the remnants in the altar cloth and dispose of the whole thing in fire. This is the easiest way to clear off an altar, but it is not the most economical. It is, however, the choice of many who make temporary cursing altars on a black cloth. Remove any valuable candle holders, bowls, or statues, then tie the cloth diagonally, "crosstownways," or "kitty cornered" around the mess, and burn it all in a bonfire or by placing it in a large iron cauldron, pouring Florida Water Cologne on it, and setting it alight. (If you contemplate doing this, plan ahead by using a natural cotton altar cloth because burning polyester or plastic is toxic!)

How often should you take down and rebuild your altars? The answer is entirely up to you. Some people never change their living room decor in fifty years; others are constantly redecorating, and the way that people dismantle and rebuild altars seems to correlate with the way they engage in home redecoration. That's why there is no one way to handle the task.

CLEANING SUPPLIES FOR THE ALTAR

Ashes will build up, wax will drip, flower vases will run out of water, offerings will go stale, and things will get dusty. Don't leave these items to the damages of time. Keep your altar clean, take care of it! By attending to it on a regular basis you will avoid problems with dirt and dust building up and taking away from the beauty of the magical space that you've created.

There are many traditional cleaning supplies used in conjure. Some can be found at grocery or drug stores; others come from candle shops. Try them out and see what you like and which products smell best to you. You may need more than one, depending on the type of items you are cleaning,

- **Chinese Wash:** The most popular product for spiritual cleansing, soap-based Chinese Wash is used to clean away messes that may have resulted from crossed conditions, jinxes, or curing enelies. It can keep the peace, help marital fidelity, and attract customers to a business.
- **Peace Water:** This is a two-layer liquid that you shake up to use. As a room spritz, it dispels negativity, brings peace, and restores harmony. It does contain oil, so it is not advised to use it directly on cloth.
- **Hoyt's Cologne:** This alcohol-based cologne is popular for feeding gambling mojos and is worn on the body for love and money. It is also an excellent room spritz for luck, money drawing, and attraction.
- **Florida Water:** This is a floral cologne with an alcohol base used for spiritual cleansing and protection. Florida Water Soap, scented with the same aroma, is good for washing delicate cloths, when added to water.
- **Buffalo Ammonia:** Likely a replacement for raw urine, Buffalo Ammonia is a cleanser that can wash away jinxes or crossed conditions.
- **13 Herb Bath:** Often used as a personal spiritual cleanser, 13 Herb Bath is also made into a tea that is used as a general wipe-down for altar surfaces. It can be added to Chinese Wash to make scrub water.
- **Pine-Sol:** This old household cleaner is a favourite in the south, especially among those whose families hail from the "Georgia pines."
- **Vinegar:** This is a great cleaner for glass, but it will ruin marble stone.
- **Lemon:** Similar to vinegar, it cuts off evil, but it will destroy marble.
- **Hydrogen Peroxide:** If you leave coffee or tea offerings out on your altar in crackle-glazed cups, they will turn brown in the cracks. Soak them in regular-strength drug store peroxide for two weeks and they will be restored. Do not use Clorox bleach — it will destroy ceramics.

1-2-3 ALTAR CLEANSING TEA WASH

This is a general altar cleansing tea that is useful for any condition:

Make 1 part Broom Straws, 2 parts Hyssop, and 3 parts Mint into a strong tea let to steep for at least fifteen minutes. Allow the water to cool completely and add 1 or 2 capfulls of Chinese Wash to the water. Use this mixture to wash your altars. It will remove any negative residue and leave your altar space totally neutral.

This is for general, generic cleansing, however, as you clean your altar space it is a good idea to really focus on the purpose of this space. Are you cleansing to create a love altar? Recite the Song of Solomon while you clean. Is your space for healing or blessing? Perhaps you offer a unique prayer from your heart. If you are creating an altar for ancestors or guides, you should spend this time talking to these spirits and let them know that you are setting up an altar for them in order to start inviting them in.

LOVE ALTAR WASH

Make a floor wash tea with a mixture of three parts Lavender, three parts Rose Petals, and one part Damiana, and wash down the surface of your love altar. Use this mixture to wash down many of the objects on your altar. Keep some as a bath for yourself to use before or after the altar is created.

MONEY ALTAR WASH

Make a tea of Alfalfa and mix it into hot water into which you have sprinkled some Money Drawing Bath Crystals. Use this mix to wash down your money altar space. Just make sure that it isn't a wooden surface or the salt in the bath crystals will dry it out.

PROTECTION ALTAR WASH

Make a tea with equal parts Rue and Hyssop and add a capfull of Chinese Wash. Use this to wash down your altar surface, as you recite the 91st Psalm.

BLESSING ALTAR WASH

Mix equal parts Blessed Thistle, chopped Angelica Root and Althæa Root. Brew it into a tea and use it to wash down your altar surfaces as you recite the 23rd Psalm. You can launder altar cloths in it as well.

ALTARS FOR ONGOING WORK

Your altar is a physical place of power, and in order to keep that power going you have to keep the battery charged. If you work at and tend to your altar on a regular basis, than this won't be a problem because you will be using the space frequently. However, if you create an altar and then just let it sit and gather dust, it won't be an effective magical tool for you.

To keep your spells ongoing while you are not standing or kneeling in front of your sanctified space, try these traditional, time-tested methods to sustain and uphold what you set in motion on the altar:

- **Prayer:** Reciting prayers or Psalms or speaking aloud your desires at your altar keeps your work ongoing. Some spells come with instructions regarding the number of times and the times of the day you are to pray. A typical recommendation is twice a day, twelve hours apart, but even if you only pray once a day, you will have helped yourself and your spiritual cause. If you have to be away from your altar, you need not stop the prayers. Continuing to pray helps to keep your focus strong.
- **Lodestones:** These minerals pull what you desire towards you. If you make an altar for love, use a pair of Lodestones; if you are drawing in money, use a single Lodestone. Be sure to feed them with Magnetic Sand regularly, to keep them alive and working for you.
- **Offerings:** If you have created a shrine for the honouring of ancestors, saints, or spirits you will need to leave fresh offerings for them. The form these offerings take will vary based on your religious, cultural, and spiritual training or the messages you receive from ancestral spirits. Renew the offerings every few days to keep them fresh.
- **Candles:** Setting lights or letting vigil candles burn continuously while you are away from the altar will keep your spell ongoing. Just be sure that you use fire safety precautions at all times when burning glass-encased candles.
- **Distributions and Donations:** Small items that have been prayed over at the altar can be distributed to others to carry your message far and wide. Marked currency and blessed coins may be given to the poor, fixed curios or trinkets may be given as gifts to anyone, and prepared food offerings left in ant hills should be accompanied by a request that the Ants carry the news of what you want all around the world.

CAT YRONWODE'S SECRETS OF ALTAR RESPECT

This was written in response to a conjure practitioner who was upset because people kept coming into her room and messing with things on her altar. One person in particular had a habit of extinguishing her altar candles. She was worried about the effect it might have on her conjure practices for her altars to be seen or touched. Miss Cat wrote as follows:

"Dear friend, i understand that people come into your private room, see the work that you are doing, want to touch or hold items that are on your altar, rearrange things, and put out your altar lights without your consent or permission. This is a form of disrespect. I am not as concerned over the effect this may have on your spells as i am concerned that it is having an effect on your sense of dignity and purpose.

"People who disrespect your altar are not good people to have in your home or in your life. You will need courage and social skills to deal with them effectively, but first it is important to understand who they are and why they are interfering with your altar.

"There are several reasons that people might disrespect your altar space. They could be folks who just don't know what you are doing or are curious about it — or their disrespect could indicate that they mean you harm or want to interrupt the work that you are doing.

"As you read the following descriptions, you will see who the various types of altar-threatening people might be and how to deal with them.

"The first step in dealing with those who have disrespected your altar is to determine what type of persons they are. This will lead you to understand how best to deal with them. The bottom line is to not allow yourself, your things, or your space to be treated with disrespect. When doing rootwork you need to protect your space and you don't need to have disrespectful people in your altar space, in your home, or in your life.

"1) Psychopaths and Sociopaths

"These are, thankfully, rare people, but we all know that the world is not perfect and that we may be exposed to psychopathic or sociopathic threats who mess with everything of anybody's; these people will rob, steal, rape, even kill with no sense of boundaries.

"*What to do?*

"Get them out of your life immediately. Do not explain, do not argue, do not attempt to influence them. Just get away.

"2) Controllers, Rulers, and Dominators

"These people are okay with society as a whole, but they want to control, rule, or dominate you specifically. They have targeted you as a victim for mental or physical abuse, parental or marital control, or domestic battering.

"What to do?

"Get them out of your life as soon as possible; this may require waiting until you come of age or can get a divorce or find a new home. Do not explain, do not argue, do not attempt to influence them. Just get away.

"3) Spiritual Haters

"These folks are okay with society and okay with you, but they believe that some or all forms of spiritual work are "wrong" or "bad" or "not real." They may hold a false belief that what you are doing is potentially "dangerous." They are only seeking to control, rule, or dominate you in this one sphere of your existence. They may believe that they have your best interest at heart.

"What to do?

"Speak directly to them and tell them to stop touching the sacred things on your altar. If they argue with you, stop the argument immediately and plan to get them out of your life as soon as possible. After your first polite request, do not engage in further conflict on the subject; do not explain, do not argue, do not attempt to influence them. Just get away.

"4) Mentally Impaired Boundary-Breakers

"These people are okay with society, okay with you, and have no opinions about your spiritual beliefs, but they are mentally ill or intoxicated in a way that renders them incognizant of boundaries. They may have OCD, ADHD, alcohol or addiction issues, or social-developmental problems that blind them to the fact that it is not okay to rummage through people's clothing, jewelry, cutlery, books, electronic equipment, or to mess with their pets or children. Their focus is not on your altar per se; in the past they might also have handled or mishandled your cell-phone, your dog, or your collection of tea-cups.

"What to do?

"Speak directly to them and tell them to stop touching the sacred things on your altar. Listen to their excuses, which might include terms like "Oh, sorry, I just couldn't help myself." Acknowledge what they say, then explain that you have rules about your altar which include no one touching it but you. If they agree to abide by the rules, clean the altar, and re-make it. Observe them the next time they visit; if they follow your rules, all is well; if they do not, consider moving them up into category 3.

"5) Hypervigilant Candle Compulsives

"These folks are okay with society and okay with you and they suffer no indoctrination by media or an organization with respect to your spiritual beliefs, and they are neither mentally ill nor intoxicated to the point that they fail to respect the property of others, but they suffer from a specific form of hypervigilant compulsivity which leads them to believe that candles are 'dangerous' and they will put candles out wherever they see them; they do this not only at your altar, but if you observe them over time you will see them do this in restaurants as well as in the homes of friends and relatives.

"What to do?

"Speak directly to them and tell them to stop touching the sacred things on your altar. Listen to their temporized excuses, which might include phrases like 'Oh, sorry, I just couldn't help myself.' When they are done talking, acknowledge what they said, then follow with a short, concise statement that you have rules about your altar which include no one touching it but you. If they say they cannot abide by the rules, because 'Candles freak me out,' or some such excuse, ask them whether they can control their impulses while in your home or if all meetings with them should be confined to rooms in which there are no burning candles. Let them explore their options. If they agree to abide by the rules, then wait until they have gone away, clean the altar, and re-make it. Observe them the next time they visit; if they follow your rules, all is well; if they do not, consider that their mental illness is such that they are not reliable and limit their ability to enter rooms in which candles are lit.

"6) Children

"They are uneducated, ignorant children.

"What to do?

"Speak directly to them and tell them to stop touching the sacred things on your altar. Be kind but firm. Use the same tone of voice you would use on a toddler who is trying to rev up a chainsaw: 'No, honey, that's a tool, not a toy. That's not yours. Put it down and let's find you some toys to play with.' Lead them out of the room, if possible. Also, if possible, give them something magical that is appropriate for a child: 'Here, honey, this is a special sacred stone from India, and you can keep it. It's for you. You can make a wish on it at night when you go to bed.'

"I believe that this list covers all the types of 'altar messers' i have ever had to deal with. You may find others, but the idea is to identify them and treat them appropriately, without losing any of your personal power."

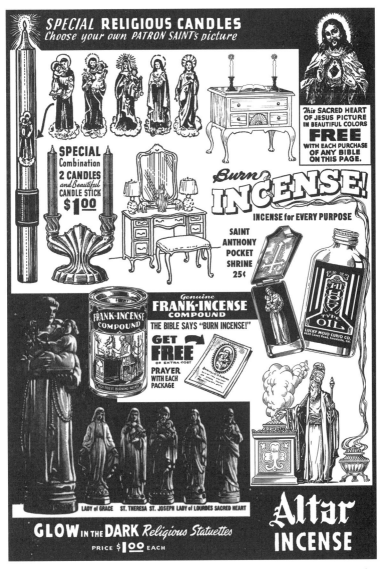

Altars and Altar Goods offered in mail order hoodoo catalogues, 1935 - 2015. Art by Charles C. Dawson, Steve Leialoha, Greywolf Townsend, and One Unknown Artist for Famous Products, Scott Foresman, and the Lucky Mojo Curio Company.

Altars for Various Conditions

An altar can be built for a wide variety of reasons. In the following pages you will find numerous altar designs for a number of conditions. In the instructions you will find a list of items you will need to create the altar, the best time to do the job, and the details on how to do it.

ALTARS FOR LOVE

Love work is the number one reason that people seek out root doctors. Love makes the world go round and we all want a piece of it. Creating an altar for love is a powerful way to bring a new love into your life, reconcile with a lost love, or increase the spark in a current love relationship.

Love altars can be created in any room of your house, but your bedroom is the most effective place to start setting up your love magic. If you have a partner and need to keep your practices secret, you can also create a small altar in a shoe box and keep it under your bed. This will help to infuse the passion in your relationship, while keeping your secret.

AN ALTAR TO ENHANCE PASSION IN A RELATIONSHIP

Create this altar space in your bedroom. The top of a dresser, a vanity, a chiffarobe, or a side table will be perfect for it. Passionate love spells are generally best if you and your lover can undertake the spells together, but love magic can also be done alone with just as much success.

Dust the altar surface with Kiss Me Now! Sachet Powder and place a red or heart-covered cloth on it. Place a vase of fresh roses or other flowers that you find beautiful and pleasingly fragrant at the center of your altar surface.

Carve your name and your lover's name on the sides of a red Lovers or bride and groom figural candle. Carve a hole in the bottom and load it with personal concerns from both of you. Sexual fluids are particularly potent, but a hair from each of you is also powerful. Melt wax over the hole to seal it.

Dress the candle with Fire of Love Oil and place it on a fire-safe surface in front of the vase of flowers. Burn the candle every Friday night to increase passion in your relationship. Replace the flowers as necessary. Once the candle burns out, set another. If you can make this a special "date night" ritual, all the better!

AN ALTAR TO BRING IN A NEW LOVE

Set this altar up on a full moon night, when you have time and can be alone. Clear and prepare a space for this spell, then lay down a red, pink, or white cloth, with or without heart-shapes printed or embroidered on it. Light Come To Me Incense in the room and let it burn the entire time that you are setting up the altar. You may add Dragon's Blood Resin to it. If you feel like it, play romantic music that creates a loving atmosphere and reminds you of feeling in love.

With the incense burning and the music playing, write out a list of what you desire in a lover, partner, or spouse. Include what the person looks like, what type of job or career he or she has, and what his or her personality is like. Take your time writing out this list; you are calling in your perfect mate here, so give this task the time and respect that it deserves.

Place a pinch of Lucky Mojo Love Herbs Mix in the center of the paper and fold it up three times, each time folding the paper towards you. Use a figural candle of the gender you want to bring into your life and dress it with Love Me Oil. Set it on one side of your altar, on top of the description of your ideal love.

Anoint a pink figural candle that matches your own gender with Come To Me Oil and place it on the opposite side of your altar space. Leading from the Love Me figural candle to your candle, lay down a line of Come To Me Sachet Powder, as if you were making a trail for the lover you are calling in to follow — a trail that leads right to you.

Light these candles for at least ten minutes every night, moving the future lover candle closer to yours each time you do, until they are so close together that you can tie them together. Don't just light the candles and walk away. As the candles burn use this time to think about the person who is hearing your call and coming to you. Focus on feelings of love and the excitement of a new relationship in your life. See that person moving closer to you and you taking him or her into your heart and into your life.

When the candles have finished burning you can divine signs or symbols in the wax that remains. These signs may include letters from the name of your love, numbers for date, and so on.

Conclude by ritually disposing of your remains at a crossroads, dropping if off and not looking back. When you return home clean up the altar space where you did the rite. Each day after the spell has been completed wear the remaining Come To Me Oil to help your new lover find you.

ALTARS FOR MONEY

The second most common reason that people seek out help from a rootworker is for money help. No matter what the specifics of the situation, this typically includes two types of work: drawing money though business, a job, inheritance, settlements, gambling, investments, freelancing, or sales, and holding on to money that's already in hand. A money altar to increase overall financial luck can help with both of these needs.

Money drawing and money keeping differ from one another, and even within the overall category of money drawing, there are disparate spells for job-getting, lottery wins, casino gambling, and insurance claims. The good thing is that you don't have to establish separate altars to perform a variety of money spells. As long as each spell you cast, each candle you light, each mojo you make, and each prayer you recite has its own specific goal, you can place all of your money and wealth work on one altar. On the other hand, if you have the space and the inclination, you can establish one altar for job and career income and another for luck at bingo or cards. The choice is yours.

AN ALL-PURPOSE MONEY ALTAR

Build this altar during a waxing moon or a full moon, especially one that is associated with money, like the full moon in Taurus. Dust the surface of your altar space with Money Drawing Sachet Powder. Over the top of the surface put a green altar cloth or an altar cloth that is covered with images of money. You may paper the altar with real dollar bills if you like.

Get a small gold-coloured dish or tray and dress it with Money Stay With Me Oil using a five-spot pattern. In the center, place a large Lodestone. You can pile up a little "nest" of coins around the Lodestone. You will need to have Magnetic Sand as well, to feed your Lodestone.

Underneath the golden dish put a bill in the largest denomination that you can afford at that moment. Next, take a green pyramid candle and engrave your name on each of its four sides, also marking it with dollar signs above and below your name. Anoint two opposite sides of the pyramid with Money Drawing Oil and the other two sides with Money Stay With Me Oil.

Each week burn some of the pyramid candle while you feed your Lodestone with Magnetic Sand and place another bill beneath the golden dish. When the pyramid finishes burning, start another one. Keep this vigil going for as long as you want to keep the money coming in and staying in.

A GAMBLING ALTAR

Create this altar when the Moon is waxing. Start by cleansing your altar surface with Lucky 13 Incense. Follow this up by placing a five-spot pattern of Lucky 13 Oil on the altar surface. Finally, lay down a gold altar cloth on which you may array coins and currency, as well as items related to the type of gambling you prefer: cards, casino chips, lottery tickets, or racing sheets.

Set two gold taper candles in the corners diagonally across from one another and two green taper candles in the other two corners. Mark the taper candles with notches so that you can burn them for seven days. In the center, between these four taper candles, set a lucky Rabbit Foot that has been lightly dressed with Van Van Oil. If you have pets who might disturb the work, then cover it with a small overturned glass bowl.

Every night that you burn the candles, sit in prayer for good luck. Ask for lucky numbers to be revealed to you for winning. During this time pay attention to any dreams, signs, or symbols that come to you. Write down any number patterns that you see and place them under the Rabbit's Foot.

After the seventh night, when the candles have burned completely, carry your fixed Rabbit's Foot with you any time that you go gambling or purchase lottery tickets. Pay attention to any numbers that you see over and over again and use these numbers for your gambling. If you placed real coins or currency on the altar, distribute them to the poor as a tithe.

A VACATION MONEY ALTAR

This altar was first offered at the 2014 Hoodoo Heritage Festival as a way to bring in "extra" money to fund a vacation or holiday.

Create a dedicated altar space; it doesn't have to be large, but use it only for this one spell. Throughout each step of the work, visualize your destination and see yourself in the areas you will visit.

Purify the surface and cover it with a green altar cloth. Place a Mercury Dime anointed with Money Drawing Oil in each corner, stating your intention (i.e.: "Take me to London."). In the center place images of your vacation destination with your petition written on them, set a money-drawing box to store your money on top of it, and start the box off with a two dollar bill inscribed with the success sigil ($$¢¢$$). Place a green 7-knob candle carved with the name of your vacation spot and dressed with Money Drawing Oil next to the box. As you work at your altar burn Crown of Success Incense. Any extra money goes directly in the box to fund your trip.

ALTARS FOR HEALING

Healing altars may be made for those who are present in the home or as distant work for clients, relatives, or friends in need.

A SIMPLE SICK-ROOM HEALING ALTAR

Brew a tea of Boneset, Coltsfoot, Self-Heal, and Life Everlasting and use it to wash down the patient's bedside table. Lay down a white handkerchief that was rinsed in Holy Water and anointed with Holy Oil. On it place a Bible open to Exodus 23:25: *"He shall bless thy bread, and thy water; and I will take sickness away from the midst of thee."* Set the patient's water glass and a small plate of food on the table and serve all food and drink to the patient from this improvised altar.

HOSPITAL HEALING ALTAR

To help someone who is in the hospital, try to create a small altar in the same room where the patient is located. If this is not possible, make an altar in your own home from which you can send distance healing to the target as a way to offer healing.

Your options are limited when you are creating an altar in a hospital room. Incense cannot be used, you can't blow any powders around, and it is unlikely that you will be able to burn candles. Modifications will have to be made to conform to hospital rules. One way to get around these roadblocks is to use stones, roots, flowers (if allowed), and other items that won't interfere with medical equipment. You will only need a small corner of a side table or a window sill.

Before going to the hospital, fix up a blue mojo bag with Althaea Herb, Life Everlasting, All Heal (Self-Heal), a quartz crystal, and a root: Queen Elizabeth for a woman or a John the Conqueror for a man. Add a healing petition in the target's name and suffumigate the mojo with Healing Incense.

At the hospital, dissolve Healing Bath Crystals from Lucky Mojo into a squirt bottle of water. Use this to wipe down the surfaces of the space where you will build the altar. This can also be used on the bars of the hospital bed, and across the threshold of the hospital room.

Take the mojo and a small LED tea light and place them on the side table that you have washed down. If the ill person is able, he or she should hold the mojo as often as possible or sleep with it under the pillow.

A SPIRITUAL CHURCH ALTAR FOR HEALING NATURE

This spell was shared by Rev. Catherine Yronwode of Missionary Independent Spiritual Church for the healing of the Gulf of Mexico after the BP Oil Spill of 2010. It can be adapted for use with any other similar environmental disaster caused by petroleum spills.

"Create an altar for the place, the people, the animals, the plants. Gather pictures, mementos, whatever helps you focus.

"Now, here is where it goes counter to what you probably thought I would suggest. DO NOT USE CANDLES ON THIS ALTAR unless they are made from 100% beeswax. Do not use petroleum based candles on this altar! In fact, I would not use any candles at all.

"Place clear glass bowls or glasses of water on the altar — I was told by Spirit to use seven of them. Glass custard cups or wine glasses will do, as long as they are clean glass with no writing or pictures on them (cut glass is okay). If possible fill them with water from seven sources (spring, river, ocean, rain, well, lake, Holy Water), but if that is too daunting, use clean spring water and ocean water mixed together.

"Set these seven bowls or glasses out in a rainbow arc on the altar. Into each bowl put a small crucifix, while speaking aloud a prayer for relief. The crucifixes may be small or large, as long as getting wet will not hurt them. Pray continually as you do this, and I recommend the 23rd Psalm and a call for help to Jesus Christ.

"Pray at this altar for three days for your specific needs in regard to the Gulf waters, the animals, the plants, and the people of the region. On the third day, take the seven bowls or glasses to the ocean and, one by one, empty them in, keeping the crucifixes, symbolically cleansing the ocean, "in the name of Jesus Christ, a fisherman, amen."

"If you do not live near the Gulf, you may pour the bowls or glasses of water into any live stream of running water, but as you empty each one, first speak aloud your understanding that all waters run to the sea, and all the seas are one, then remove the crucifix, and say your prayer for cleansing the ocean, "in the name of Jesus Christ, a fisherman, amen."

"The seven crucifixes may be gifted to seven friends with instructions for this rite, in the expectation that each of them will acquire six more crucifixes and do the same, and thus spread the rite around the world, or, if you prefer, the crucifixes may be given to those in need of spiritual help in this time of crisis."

ALTARS FOR PROTECTION

Protection altars are generally discreet or hidden in plain sight.

A HOME PROTECTION MIRROR ALTAR
To stop evil before it enters, hang a prepared mirror in an entrance hall or foyer, facing the front door. A flat manila envelope is taped to the back of the mirror. Inside are a copy of the 91st Psalm, the names of family members, herbs and roots like Rue, Angelica, Mint, and Devil's Shoe String, and an image of Jesus Christ placed so that it faces outward, toward the doorway.

A HOME PROTECTION WALL ALTAR
A wall shelf or a Mexican nicho makes a fine protection altar. If it contains a mirror at the back and holds a few decorative containers of protective herbs, no one will be the wiser. A cluster of reed diffusers or Bamboo fragrance sticks dipped in Fiery Wall of Protection Oil, amidst which you have placed nine lengths of Devil's Shoe String completes the layout nicely.

A MOTHER'S GUIDING LIGHT FOR HER CHILDREN
Catherine Yronwode shares this old-time protection altar spell:

"If you have a young one in need of protection, make your protective altar look like an everyday knick-knack display, hiding it in plain site.

"Purchase a Guardian Angel statue. Write the child's name and birth date on a slip of paper or a small photo and tape a hair of the child to it. Go to a crafts store and buy green or brown crafter's felt and glue. Glue the prepared paper face-up to the statue, then glue the felt on. Pray Psalms 91 as you work. Trim the felt to the base of the statue; no one will know what is under the felt.

"Get an easel frame for a photo of the child and behind the photo, when you put it in the frame, insert two papers. On the first paper write out your prayer for the child's safety and happiness. On the second paper write out a copy of Psalms 91 in your own handwriting. You may add a pinch each of these three herbs: Angelica Root Powder, Motherwort, and Althaea Leaf.

"Assemble the photo with the hidden papers in the frame. Place the Guardian Angel statue and the framed photo of the child on a book case, entertainment center shelf, or small table-top. Set a floral array and a simple white candle dressed with Protection Oil in front of the display. Burn the candle when the child may be away from home or in any kind of danger."

ALTARS FOR JUSTIFIED ENEMY WORKS

An altar for justified work against enemies is usually created for one-time use and taken down when the job is finished, unless the person who makes it is a professional who serves clients in need of such services. After doing any type of enemy work, even justified spells for justice, wash down the altar, take a spiritual bath with Hyssop, and Recite Psalms 51.

HOT FOOT TERRIBLE NEIGHBOURS ALTAR
Face this altar so that you stand at it looking in the direction of the terrible neighbour's house or turn your body to face the neighbour's house as you work. Do this spell during a waning moon on a Saturday or Tuesday.

Wipe the surface with Van Van Oil and lay down a red cloth or a black bandana with a print of Red Chili Peppers. Sprinkle or blow Hot Foot Powder onto the cloth. Write out the names of your neighbours or their address, and all across it, in every direction, write commands like "get out," "move away," and "vacate your house." Inscribe their names or address on a red offertory candle, dress it with Hot Foot Oil, and roll it in Red Pepper Flakes or Powder. Use a stamped metal star candle holder for the candle because you will dispose of it at the end of the spell. Recite Psalms 1 and speak your prayer for the neighbours to get out. Let the candle burn down, and when it is done, wrap everything up in the altar cloth, making a small, tight bundle, and leave it in your neighbour's front yard or on their doorstep without being seen. If possible tuck it into a plant or fence corner where it won't be found. Once they move out, dispose of the bundle in running water.

MISS CAT'S JUSTICE ALTAR IN A POLICE SHOOTING CASE
On the wall or in easel frames place pictures of seven people who died fighting for justice, such as John Brown, Rev. George Lee, Lamar Smith, Medgar Evers, James Earl Chaney, Andrew Goodman, Michael Henry Schwerner, and Martin Luther King, Jr. — or your choice. Inscribe each name in a spiral on a white candle. Dress the candles with 7-11 Holy Oil. Write out by hand Psalms 109: *"Hold not thy peace, O God of my praise..."* with the name of the policeman who did wrong wherever it says "he" or "him" in the Psalm. Upon the paper set the seven candles in the form of a cross. Burn the candles in sections over seven days, in the name of Jesus Christ.

```
    O
  O O O
    O
    O
    O
```

ALTARS FOR CURSING AND VENGEANCE

Altars for cursing and vengeance are rarely kept permanently except by professionals who take on clients. For occasional cursing work it is best to create a temporary altar. Once the job is done, clean the area thoroughly and take a Hyssop bath while reciting Psalms 51. Don't keep that stuff hanging around you any longer than necessary.

LITTLE COFFIN ALTAR

Use an altar of this kind to lock up an enemy. Start with a small coffin-shaped box. It can be made out of any wood or ceramic, but pine is preferred. Line the interior of the box with mirrors to further trap the target and reflect their actions and misery back at them.

Create this altar at night during the dark of the Moon. Lay down a black altar cloth and place the little coffin in its center. Place a black candle dressed with an appropriate oil on each side of the coffin, light them, and sprinkle equal parts Red Pepper flakes and Asafoetida into the bottom of the coffin.

Next make a doll baby in the name of your enemy and place it in the coffin on top of the herb mixture. Add a few more pinches of the herb mixture on top of the doll-baby. State your intentions as you put the lid on the coffin and wrap it tightly with Knotweed. Burn a dressed black candle on top of the coffin each night for three nights. On the last night once the candle is done gather up all the items and bury them in a graveyard. Upon your return, immediately clean your altar space and bathe with Hyssop.

BREAK UP TOILET ALTAR

This is one of the most basic altars, but it is also one of the most potent. To do it, first create a vinegar jar for the two people whom you wish to split up. A Break Up Spell Kit from Lucky Mojo will have the items and instructions needed for this work if you are not comfortable creating it on your own.

Create the jar at night and take the completed jar to your bathroom. Place the jar on the back of the toilet on top of the tank. Excrement flows out through your toilet every day, and by placing the jar here you are keeping it near this potent negativity. Once a day go to this altar space and shake the jar vigorously to agitate the relationship that you intend to break up.

Shrines of Veneration

ANCESTOR ALTARS

Ancestor veneration abounds in cultures throughout the world. Many people believe that to remember, honour, and pay homage to one's ancestors helps their spirits thrive. In some traditions failure to honour your ancestors can prompt them to act maliciously toward you.

Once you establish an ancestor altar you can begin to petition your ancestors to aid you and help connect to your roots. Remember, no matter who your ancestors were in life or where they came from, all those who came before you helped contribute to you being in this world. If you cannot work with an immediate ancestor due to your relationship while they were living, it is better to choose a more distant ancestor than with none at all.

Your ancestor altar can be as simple or as elaborate as you desire. It can include pictures, mementos, candles, and lamps. The one component of the altar that is an absolute necessity is an offering space.

A SIMPLE ANCESTOR ALTAR

Start by cleaning your chosen space. This can be a desk, an end table, a mantel, or a bookshelf. Place one or more framed photos of your ancestors in the center of the space or on the wall behind it. Set a small tea light and a shallow dish of Kananga Water in front of the photo. The Kananga Water will evaporate over time, so check the dish frequently, and refill it as necessary. Burn a new candle whenever you want to communicate with your ancestor and as you feel the urge to honour them.

AN ELABORATE ANCESTOR ALTAR

Start your space as with the simple ancestor altar, but place an altar cloth down first. Material once owned by your ancestor such as articles of their clothing or linens makes for a potent altar cloth. If you do not have access to such articles, then a plain, clean, white cloth is acceptable. Once you have your space prepared, you can add as much as your heart desires or as much as your ancestors ask for. Our ancestors are unique, so their altars should also be unique. An elaborate ancestor altar should reflect who they were and who you are through them.

HOW TO PERFORM AN ANCESTRAL ELEVATION

Ancestral Elevation is a nine-day rite performed by members of the religion of Kardecian Spiritism. Its aim is to help spirits of the dead progress in their evolution to higher planes of existence. This brief summary is based on the more extensive instructions by Khi Armand:

Through intercession and words of comfort, an Ancestral Elevation helps transport the departed from the physical plane to the ancestral realms. It can be performed for specific ancestors, for all of one's ancestors, and for spirits of the dead to whom you are not biologically related. It can be changed according to the traditions important to the spirits who are being elevated.

For this work you will need a white altar cloth, one large white candle, eight sturdy books or bricks, a glass of clean water, and a pleasant-smelling incense, such as Blessing, Healing, Spirit Guide, Indian Spirit Guide, Frankincense, Myrrh, Tobacco, Sweet Grass, or Althæa Root chips. Dress your candle with Blessing, Healing, or Tranquility Oil.

First, place a book or brick on a clean surface and spread the white cloth on top. Place the glass of water at the center and add white flowers or religious items that would be comforting to the souls you are elevating. If the altar includes photos of the deceased ensure that no photos of the living are present. Set the candle on the altar and light it along with your incense, burning both as an offering to any benevolent spirits who arrive to offer aid and comfort to those whom you are elevating. Prayerfully ask your Guiding Spirits to aid in helping these souls let go of what is holding them back, then offer up traditional prayers or songs that would be comforting to those you are elevating, such as Psalms 23, "Amazing Grace," or the Our Father. Imagine your voice as a sound bridge connecting these souls from the plane they are on to the plane it would best serve them to reach. Then thank your Helping Spirits for their protection and aid and snuff out your candle.

The next day, dismantle the altar, place a second book or brick on the clean surface. Reassemble your altar on top and perform the service again. Repeat the rite, adding a book or brick each day. At the end of nine days, you may perform divination on the effects of your work.

You can read more about ancestor altars and Ancestor Elevation in:
"Deliverance!" by Khi Armand
For more on Kardecian Spiritism, see this web page at AIRR:
ReadersAndRootworkers.org/wiki/Category:Working_Within_the_Spiritualist_Tradition

ALTARS FOR CATHOLIC SAINTS

Catholic-style altars are created to venerate the saints in order to ask for their aid as intercessors between a supplicant and God.

A saint is a human being who has been called to holiness or has, consciously or unconsciously, fulfilled the criteria set for sainthood by a religious institution. More than 10,000 saints have been formally canonized by the Roman Catholic church. In addition, the Vatican recognizes the Jewish hierarchy of angels and archangels as saints, and there are numerous folk saints beloved by the laity but unrecognized by the church.

However, not all altars that display Catholic iconography, statuary, or saint pictures necessarily belong to Catholic practitioners. For instance, as documented by the African-American film director and photographer Gordon Parks on behalf of the Farm Security Administration of the U.S. Government, members of the Black Spiritual Church Movement often kept statuettes of Catholic saints on their altars. In 1942 Parks photographed Ella Watson, a Black government charwoman who lived in Washington, D.C. and was a member of a Spiritualist Christian church.

Spiritualism developed as an independent religious movement in the mid-19th century, drawing its membership from both Protestant and Catholic denominations. The church that Watson attended, Saint Martin's, honoured Saint Martin de Porres, the first Black Catholic saint. It drew its inspiration and many of its adherents from the Catholic church, while presenting Spiritualist rituals such as flower services, foot washings, and the laying on of hands by female clergy. Ella Watson's household vanity-top altar, with its statues of Saint Theresa, Our Lady of Grace, and Saint Martin de Porres, might easily have been mistaken for a Catholic altar, except that it also featured two lucky trunk-up white Elephants, a Bible, and seven candlesticks laid out in the shape of a cross.

When creating an altar for a saint or saints, start by placing a statue, holy card, or medallion of the saint at the center of your space. Take the time to make this a beautiful area that encourages the saint to come to aid you. Research the saint's preferred offerings, colours, days of the week, and yearly feast-days, then use that information to make your altar all the more pleasing. Renew your floral arrangements, candles, and offerings regularly, and you will be well on your way to having a lovely devotional altar for your chosen saint.

MAKING OFFERINGS TO SPIRITS

Creating an altar for an ancestor, Catholic saint, deity, or other spirit is the first step toward the work that you will do with those entities. Once you have an altar established you can begin to develop an ongoing relationship with these spirits. It is important that you continue to interact with the spirit at your altar, leaving offerings and spending time with the entities whom you have called upon.

Spending time at your altar doesn't have to have a specific set of actions to it, and there isn't one ritual, activity, or initiation that you need to know about for your altar to be effective. Just keep in mind that you have invited a spiritual being into your life and into your home. Treat that spirit like you would any corporeal person. Don't ignore the spirit-being's energy and don't forget it is there. Treat nonphysical entities with proper behaviour, and expect the same from them. Honour them by taking time with them. The more you sit with your altar, the more you will begin to hear and understand the messages that these entities may be sending to you.

So how do you plan on working at this space? Are you setting vigil candles? Are you burning incense? Are you doing anything with Magnetic Sand, Lodestones, magnets, or powders? Are you sitting in meditation? Are you reciting prayers and Psalms? Are you calling out the names of your ancestors? Are you laying out plates of food, glasses of water, wine, liquor or other libations?

Remember that every time you light a candle, every time you ignite some incense, every time you set down a glass of water, you are helping to feed the entity that you have invited into your home. Take these steps seriously and give the spirit the attention and reverence that it, and any entities whose alliance you seek, deserve.

In addition to burning candles or lamps, you can also include such offerings as a small dish of Kananga Water, Florida Water, whiskey, or a drink your ancestor or the spirit favours. A cigar or cigarette, a pinch of chewing Tobacco, or snuff can be offered, as well as favoured candies, sweets, or flowers. Some saints prefer traditional food offerings such as breads or cakes. Don't allow the food, candies, liquids, or flowers to spoil. If your altar is inviting and pleasing to your ancestors, saints, deities, or spirits, then they will be more inclined to visit it, to look upon you favourably, and to aid you when you call on them.

Unusual Altars

TRAVELLING ALTARS

Altars need not be stationary. Travelling altars can be created for special events or as opportunities to lay tricks that can't be done at home. They can be designed for one-time use or carried with you all the time. They can be constructed for general spell-casting or for specific situations.

DOCTOR'S BAG OR VANITY CASE AS TRAVELLING ALTAR
It is not unusual for root doctors to make house calls for in-person work, spiritual house cleaning, or hands-on healing, and professionals who travel to their clients usually carry a latched case or bag filled with the items they need when on call. A travelling work box can become a travelling altar if the conjurer employs it as such in the client's home or place of business.

Many professional rootworkers use medical doctor's bags or ladies' suitcase-style vanity cases as travelling altars. The bags or cases contain supplies for house calls and they also hold everything needed to set up an altar, much after the manner of a Catholic priest's sick-call set.

Mail order hoodoo shops carry fully stocked bags and cases complete with altar cloths, candles, candle-stands, oils, incenses, powders, washes, colognes, and the Book of Psalms. To assemble your own, search for "vintage leather doctor bag" or "vintage leather vanity case" online or find them at antique fairs or shops. High-end doctor's bags have built-in layers and compartments that allow you to stack, store, and separate your supplies to keep them organized. Vanity cases contain a mirror and may have fold-out trays on which statuary and candles can be arrayed. Clean vintage bags and cases with metal bumper corners and operational clasps are pricey, but they are well worth the cost. They are also still being manufactured, if you prefer a new one.

Rev. Catherine Yronwode offers this advice on filling your bag or case: "Coloured handkerchiefs make excellent altar cloths. Don't forget to include matches and star holders for your candles. Joss sticks and incense matches weigh less than incense braziers. Purple flannel Crown Royal whiskey bags keep glass bottles from clinking together. Keep herbs and powders in containers with secure lids or stoppers. Include a pendulum or cards for divination. A smart phone or ipad can supply an image of a saint or a deity."

SHE SAID YES LOVE TRAVEL ALTAR

This is a great altar to take with you on a romantic weekend or vacation when you are planning to pop the question. Use this altar to help set the mood in a bedroom and enhance a sensual atmosphere. For this travelling altar you will need a cigar box or a box of a similar size.

Start by dusting the empty box with Kiss Me Now and Marriage Sachet Powder. Pack the following items in the box: a package of dried Rose Petals, a red cloth handkerchief, three stamped metal star candle holders, three four-inch chime candles (red, pink, and white), a red bride and groom candle, a bottle of Marriage Oil, a bottle of Love Me Oil, a small metal dish, self-lighting charcoal disks, a needle, and a packet of Love Me Incense.

When you arrive in your romantic spot, take your materials out of the box and set up your altar. Using the empty box to form the base of your altar, drape the red handkerchief over the box. Anoint the bride and groom figural candle with Marriage Oil and place it at the far back of the altar space. Inscribe both of your names onto each of the three candles with the needle, writing the names around in spirals. Anoint the candles with Love Me Oil, and place them in a triangle around the dish so that it sits in the center of the altar. Light a charcoal disk and sprinkle a small amount of the incense on it. As the incense smokes, light the three chime candles. While they burn, hold the dried Rose Petals in your cupped hands and pray over them that you will receive the "yes" that you are hoping for. Sprinkle the Rose Petals over the bed and prepare for a great weekend.

HEALING TRAVEL ALTAR

This altar takes into account the fact that when visiting a friend in a hospital recovery room you will not be able to employ flammable materials such as candles or incense. Decorate a cigar box and use it to store your items for easy transport. In the box pack a small bottle containing fresh water into which you have dissolved a small amount of Healing Bath Crystals, a packet of Healing Sachet Powder, a blue handkerchief, and a statuette of Dr. Jose Gregorio Hernandez. If the illness is dire, add a statuette of Saint Jude.

Sprinkle the sachet powder on the surface where you will be setting out the altar. Place the cigar box on the space and drape the handkerchief over it. Anoint the statuary with the healing water, place it in the center of the altar, and pray for Dr. Jose Gregorio Hernandez to aid the medical staff and, if the case is despaired of, for Saint Jude's miraculous intercession.

POCKET ALTARS

Pocket altars, also known as pocket shrines, are so small that they fit in a pocket or purse. You can take them with you anywhere, anytime.

Pocket shrines are not new. They have a long history, and we have examples of pocket shrines sold in Chicago-based hoodoo catalogues as early as 1936, such as the pocket shrine to Saint Anthony. This was a gold-plated, engine-turned steel cigarette-case-style container in which was fixed a celluloid plastic statuette of the saint. Others pocket altars of this time period were made of plastic, with sliding doors, and contained bas-relief inserts of the Holy Family or small statuettes of other saints.

If you know what to look for, you can find or make altars in cigarette cases, ring boxes, business card holders, mint tins, or matchboxes. These small altars can be carried with you while you travel away from home and your regular altars. You may have never seen someone with a pocket altar or pocket shrine, and that is their beauty; you can keep them private.

A pocket altar isn't the same as a mojo. The outer layer of a mojo is usually made of soft leather or fabric, whereas a pocket shrine will have sturdy, solid sides. A mojo is a magical object that you feed and keep hidden from others, while a pocket altar can be seen by others when you wish. Finally, a mojo is intended to address a specific wish or condition, but a pocket altar will generally be dedicated to an ancestor, saint, deity, or other spiritual entity.

SAFE TRAVEL POCKET ALTAR

Start with a little tin box, like a mint tin. Acquire a small figurine that matches the mode of transportation that you will be using; such as a car, train, plane, or ship, and make sure that it will fit comfortably in the tin.

The first step in building this altar is to sprinkle Safe Travel Sachet Powder and some dried Mint inside of the box, covering as much of the inside of the tin container as you can. Then lay some simple white fabric, such as from a pocket handkerchief, inside the tin. Affix the white fabric into the corners of the tin using a hot glue gun. Once the white fabric is secured in place and the glue is dry, the creative process of this altar starts.

Dust the figure of your mode of transport with Safe Travel Sachet Powder and glue it into the tin, along with several small pictures of the destination of your travels. Then pray over the tin for a safe journey and carry the pocket altar on your person, in your glove box, or in your luggage.

FIND A NEW LOVE POCKET ALTAR

Start with a small mint tin, a scrap of pink fabric, and Attraction Sachet Powder. Dress the tin with the sachet powder and write a petition paper describing the person you want to bring into your life. Roll up the petition paper and place it in the tin. Glue the pink fabric into the box on top of the petition paper to create a soft lining. You can use this altar to help draw someone by taking a small pair of Lodestones, naming them after yourself and the person you want to draw to you or the characteristics of the person you want to draw to you. Dress your Lodestone with Come To Me Oil, and dress the other with Attraction Sachet Powder. Wrap the Lodestones together with red fabric and put them in the tin. Feed the Lodestones with Magnetic Sand and dust the altar with Damiana and Rose Petals. Take this altar with you when you go places where you might meet a new love, the glove box of your car, for instance.

POCKET SHRINE IN A MATCHBOX

The idea of a matchbox shrine is just like the other pocket shrines, but on an even smaller scale. A matchbox shrine is tiny! Luckily, as the interest in matchbox shrines has grown, so has the interest in scrapbooking, which means that you can now walk into any craft store and find hundreds of miniature decorative items that fit perfectly in matchbox shrines and can be used for a wide range of conditions. Seasonal and holiday items are especially good for creating the proper atmosphere. Dollhouse-sized furniture and accessories can turn a matchbox into a tiny diorama for any sort of condition altar. When creating a tiny shrine, your creativity is the only limit!

SAINT ALTAR IN A BUSINESS CARD HOLDER

If you would like a pocket altar to the saint of your choice, take a business card holder that opens on the short end, so that the saint card, which is usually printed vertically, can be placed right side up in the erect half of the business card holder. This will leave the other half of the holder as the flat surface of the altar, where you can burn incense matches as an offering to the saint for whom the altar is built. Petition papers can also be written out and placed behind the saint card, or under a birthday candle that is lit and set on the altar surface. Other offerings can be placed in the altar as long as they fit within the space.

PROF. PORTERFIELD'S PORTABLE POCKET ALTAR

This unique altar by Professor Porterfield comes from the old folklore belief that a deck of cards can serve as Bible, almanac, and prayer book.

For this altar you need a deck of playing cards, a Sharpie marker, and a handkerchief. Use your Sharpie marker to write the following on the cards, leaving the Sevens, Nines, and Jacks blank:

- **Aces:** Hearts - Life, Diamonds - God, Clubs - Devil, Spades - Death.
- **Twos:** Hearts - the Old Testament, Diamonds - the New Testament, Clubs – the Bible, Spades – the Beginning and End.
- **Threes:** Hearts – Your Own Name, Diamonds – Father, Clubs - Son, Spades - the Holy Ghost.
- **Fours:** Hearts - Matthew, Diamonds - Mark, Clubs - Luke, Spades - John.
- **Fives:** Hearts, Diamonds - Wise Virgins, Clubs, Spades - Foolish Virgins.
- **Sixes:** Hearts - Day and Night, Diamonds - Sky and Land, Clubs - Sun and Moon, Spades - Birds and Beasts.
- **Eights:** Hearts - Noah, Diamonds - Noah's wife, Clubs - Noah's Sons, Spades - Noah's Daughters.
- **Tens:** Hearts, Diamonds – Thou Shalt, Clubs, Spades – Thou Shalt Not.
- **Queens:** Hearts - Eve, Diamonds – Bathsheba, Clubs - Queen of Sheba, Spades - Virgin Mary.
- **Kings:** Hearts - Adam, Diamonds – King David, Clubs - Solomon, Spades – Joseph the Carpenter.

The completed cards now give you all of creation and the Bible for your altar. The blank Sevens negatively and blank Nines positively represent Love, Wealth, Work, and Troubles respective to Hearts, Diamonds, Clubs, and Spades. The blank Jacks represent any individual you wish to aid, pray for, throw roots on, draw closer, or even curse.

To use this altar lay out the handkerchief as an altar cloth and then place any four marked cards in the corners of the cloth for veneration, meditation, or to be called upon. In the center of your cloth you will lay out whichever Sevens, Nines, or Jacks you are working on or for. You can even deal the cards out at random to use this altar for divination. When finished put the cards back in the pack and tie the handkerchief around it.

You can read more about playing cards in hoodoo and conjure in:
"A Deck of Spells" by Professor Charles Porterfield

HIDDEN ALTARS

From the injunction to keep a mojo hid to working sneaky tricks for magical purposes, hiding one's spiritual spells is a common practice in hoodoo, especially among those who are seeking to influence people in a shared household and do not wish their work to be known.

Hidden altars are those that are concealed in an everyday place, such as a water heater closet, broom closet or hollow book. They may be erected inside of a file cabinet, far back on the top shelf of a china hutch, behind a toilet, under the sink, on top of the refrigerator, under the bed, in a drawer, up inside the fireplace, under the stairs, inside a bureau, behind a loose piece of wall, or even in a garden shed. Sometimes you need to keep your altar hidden yet still have the work continue. A hidden altar allows you to do this.

Hidden altars may also be crafted as sacred spaces in a similar way to travelling, in that you take them down daily so no one knows that you are doing any work at all. A classic example of a take-down hidden altar is one created by a person who lives in shared space with roommates and keeps all of his altar paraphernalia in an innocuous paper bag, wrapping it all up and tucking it away until it's safe to pull everything back out again.

Altars hidden in plain sight take on the appearance of something else so that they do not look like an altar at all. Hiding an altar in plain sight involves making it look innocuous to the casual observer. Dressing or loading a few porcelain knick-knacks with protection curios and leaving them out on a shelf or table, having a potted plant at your front door with a few items hidden in the dirt and a small "cute" saint statue in the pot, a Bible left open to a specific page of scripture on your dresser, or a set of pictures of deceased loved ones or family members on the fireplace mantel with a glass of water. These are all altars hidden in plain sight.

The best hidden in plain sight altars are the ones that look like you added a simple decorative touch to your home. If you live with people and you don't want them to know what kinds of altars you keep or the nature of your spiritual practices, if you have people often coming and going through your space, or if an altar in your home would seem totally out of place, an altar hidden in plain sight may be just what you need.

The nice thing about both hidden altars and altars hidden in plain sight is that every time you walk by that altar you will know what it is for and will naturally focus your thoughts, wishes, desires, and prayers on it.

HIDDEN ALTARS OF THE SLAVERY ERA

Archaeologists have found hidden altars on the East Coast of the United States on properties where slaves were once held. In Maryland, their digs have uncovered several homes where altars were hidden under bricks in the floor, under entryways, and inside of chimneys and fireplaces. African-style floor altars were still commonplace in those days, and a room in which loose floor bricks concealed caches of sacred items were, in essence, an altar.

It is clear as well, from information handed down through folkloric and family sources, that slaves who laboured inside the home not only had access to areas where hidden altars could be placed, they actually created and hid such altars. Their altars were places where active resistance was engaged against a master or mistress and prayers were made for escape and deliverance. Hollow candlesticks, Staffordshire mantelpiece figurines, and other places where folks would not think to look had items hidden in them. Many of these altars and the rituals performed at them have been lost to time through disuse and age, as well as being overlooked because they were, in fact, hidden. We don't tend to hold on to the past in the United States, especially when that past is reprehensible, but it is part of our history, and it is a part of hoodoo.

Start looking around when you visit other people's homes and job sites; keep an eye out for altars hidden in plain sight. They are all over the place, much more than you might believe. These altars are so common because they can be used no matter what the living situation is or what condition is being working on.

HIDDEN CURSING ALTAR

A favourite type of hidden altar is made to hold curses that are performed in a vinegar jar in the bathroom. The jar is left down low on the floor, behind the toilet. All of the "crap" literally goes by it every time you flush. The work absorbs negativity all day.

HIDDEN LOVE ALTAR

Love altars are often hidden under the bed. The simplest way to practice at this type of altar is to store it in a container and push it under the bed, then pull it out and work with it as often as needed. Between working times, it is returned to its resting place, leaving no evidence that there is an altar or any spells being cast in the bedroom.

GODDESS MOJO'S HIDDEN TRAY ALTARS

Small trays make excellent portable altars. These were described on the Lucky Mojo Forum by a woman who calls herself Goddess Mojo:

"Tray altars can be picked up and moved around without disturbing the ongoing jobs, and can also be easily put away. They are handy for moving from room to room if you are watching the spells as you go. Mini oil lamps are useful with these portable altars because the light can be turned down low and hidden in a cabinet for short amounts of time.

"My love altar is small, perhaps six inches around. It's a black 1930s tin tray with Roses painted on it. The tray holds a red oil lamp, crystal skulls representing myself and my lover, a few love tokens, a small incense holder — the type with space for both cone and stick incense — a vase for offerings, a statue of the Roman deity Luna and her twins, and a candle, and there is still room for whatever I am trying to do at the time. It sits on one bedside table and easily hides inside of the cabinet with one motion. I use a similar tray for my money altar, which is on the other table. It's far easier to move a $20.00 bill surrounded by dimes and powders with a candle on top in one single move via the tray."

Goddess Mojo explains that when creating an altar on a tray, you can add items such as a plant or a family photo to disguise the nature of the altar and to hide it from the untrained eye. Decorative wooden boxes or cigar boxes are useful to hold supplies as well as to double as small, portable altars. Boxes with latches are particularly effective in discouraging nosy people from prying into what is inside. To use a decorative box as an altar, remove the supplies held inside of it, drape an altar cloth over the top, and place a candle, statue, or whatever items you were keeping inside on top of it. Then you will have what she calls a "temporary altar, easily moveable while keeping work intact."

Tea lights are ideal for these portable altars because they are small, readily available, and easily dressed for your enchantments. Goddess Mojo adds that "tea lights are also great because you can pop the tea light out of the metal tin, put your herbs, oils, and petition in the tin, and put the candle back on top." They burn quickly, which is perfect for small tasks or jobs that need to be repeated for several evenings in a row.

If privacy is at a premium for you, definitely consider creating altars on small trays and using lidded boxes to store your paraphernalia. This box can double as altar pedestals when you put the altars into use.

HIDDEN IN PLAIN SIGHT PROTECTION ALTAR

Here is an altar work to be left out in plain sight to aid you with personal protection. To create this altar you will need the following items: a large decorative glass jar, coloured round marbles or flat glass gems, Protection Bath Crystals, Protection Oil, salt, a large white offertory candle, and a small square of clean, white paper.

To begin the process of creating this altar, first wash the glass jar and the marbles in a bath made up with Protection Bath Crystals and salt. As the marbles soak write out your petition for who or what you want protection from onto the square of clean, white paper. Leave the jar and marbles to dry overnight. The next morning place your petition in the bottom of the dry glass and fill up the jar with the coloured marbles or glass gems. Anoint the candle with Protection Oil and place it in on top of the glass gems in the jar. Light the candle daily and replace it as needed. Wash the jar and glass gems in the Protection Bath as often as it feels necessary, about as often as you do a spiritual cleansing.

HIDDEN IN PLAIN SIGHT LOVE ALTAR

This is an altar used to keep a romantic relationship strong and solid. It can be hidden in plain sight on a bedside table, nearby shelf, or right on the headboard if you have a wide or a bookshelf style headboard. Because this altar isn't an obvious one, you can use it to work on your current lover without them ever knowing what you're up to.

To create this altar you will need the following items: a picture frame, a photo of you and your lover, Love Me Sachet Powder, Love Me Oil, and a red candle the size and shape of your choosing.

Start by writing out a petition paper on the back of the photo that names your lover and lays out what you want from them and your relationship. I suggest a heart-shaped petition written without lifting your pen. Dust the empty picture frame and the photograph with Love Me Sachet Powder. Place the photograph in the frame and say a heart-felt prayer for your relationship to be loving and long lasting, as well as any other outcomes you desire for the two of you. Stand the framed photograph up on your chosen space. Dress the candle with Love Me Oil and place it by the picture. Light the candle as you concentrate again on your desired outcome. Burn the candle any time you make love with your partner, replacing it with a new candle as needed.

BUSINESS AND OFFICE ALTARS

There are a number of tricks in hoodoo and conjure to help a business prosper and thrive, as well as to draw in new customers and income. To be truly effective, these should be cast at the site where the money is needed, not at one's home. Keeping a permanent altar in a shop or office not only aids in drawing money, clients, success, and prosperity to the enterprise; you can also do spells to maintain peace between co-workers and keep away troubled customers or the law.

You might be thinking that you've never seen an altar in a place of business before, but you'd be wrong. Consider this: How many times have you walked into a shop and seen the first dollar that the business earned from a customer framed and hanging on a wall? I bet you've seen this many times and in a variety of types of businesses. Although this might not be obvious at first glance, it is an altar picture as well as a spell to draw business and prosperity to the store. Most of these shop owners may not think of that dollar as altar decor, but that is exactly what it is!

Now imagine if you were to dress that dollar with Money Drawing Oil or Sachet Powder and write out a petition on the back of the picture frame or on the back of the dollar. What might look like innocuous business tradition turns into a strong hoodoo Money Drawing altar in plain sight right on the wall of your business.

Business owners aren't the only ones who can use rootwork to improve working conditions. Casting spells in an office environment can help co-workers get along better, reduce gossip and jealousy, and create a peaceful atmosphere. If you have a full-time job, you are spending more hours during the week with your co-workers than you are at home. Creating a happy and positive work place is important to our well-being.

An altar in your office can help you receive a promotion, get a raise, improve productivity, and aid your decision-making abilities, as well as your general luck and success. It can bring about better relations with your boss or help sway your boss to favour you. An office altar doesn't have to be big, elaborate, or ornate, especially when that isn't possible due to limitations on space. Keep it simple and watch your workplace change.

Even if you are in an office where personal items aren't allowed, you can still dress your desk, keyboard, chair, and cubicle to help create a more positive professional environment.

BUSINESS ALTAR FOR INCREASING INCOME

If you own or run a business, one of the simplest altars you can make is in or by your cash register. The cash register becomes the altar itself to help draw in more customers, prosperity, and money.

The layout for this altar is an old but simple one. You will need the following items for it: a small dish, a large Lodestone, Magnetic Sand, Prosperity Bath Crystals, Prosperity Sachet Powder, and Prosperity Oil.

Clear out a small space under or next to your cash register or use one of the small cubbies inside it. This space needs to be large enough to accommodate the small dish with the Lodestone sitting on it.

Start by taking out any cash in the register and wiping the register with a spiritual cleanser, such as Florida Water or diluted Chinese Wash. Dissolve the Prosperity Bath Crystals into a spray bottle of fresh water. Spray the cash register with the Prosperity water, inside and out. Keep the spray at a fine mist so the machine doesn't get wet, and let it air dry completely.

Dust the paper money and coins with the Prosperity Sachet Powder. Throughout this process focus on drawing in new clients ready to spend money coming into your shop. Envision your location as a magnet that is drawing in generous clients, prosperity, success, and wealth.

Anoint the Lodestone with the Prosperity Oil, all the while speaking to the Lodestone, telling it that its job is to draw customers and money to your business. You may give it a name, if you wish. Many people name their business Lodestones and treat them as they would a working animal.

Write out a petition on a dollar bill describing your perfect prospective customer and how much money you want to see coming in. Then write your own name under the name of the Secretary of the Treasury on the front of the bill and the $$¢¢$$ Sigil on all four edges of the bill. Place your petition under the dish with some currency and put the Lodestone in the dish. This makes a little "nest" for the Lodestone to sit in and hatch more money. Set the dish in your cash register, under it, or next to it. Feed the Lodestone with Magnetic Sand. Return the rest of the coins and cash to your register, except for a few coins, which you give to the Lodestone. Take a moment to pray for your business to become a success that draws in customers and ever increasing prosperity. The 23rd Psalm is a good prayer if you need one.

Each day give a coin from the Lodestone dish away in change to a good customer, then feed your Lodestone a pinch of Magnetic Sand, a drop of Prosperity Oil, and a new coin, and say a silent prayer.

OFFICE ALTAR FOR PROMOTION

A simple office altar can fit on the corner of your desk, in a desk drawer, or even into the frame of a picture to help keep it completely hidden. Some corporations have rules about what you can have on your desk, so adjust your altar to fit your corporate environment and its potential restrictions.

If you want to get promoted, whether there is a promotion available or not, build this altar in your office, on your desk, or in your work cubicle to help enhance your chances for success and recognition.

Start by writing out a petition for a promotion on a clean, square piece of paper. If possible, do this while on the job and at your desk, during a time that you will be free from interruption. Anoint a small Lodestone with Crown of Success Oil and feed it a pinch of Magnetic Sand while stating your desire for a promotion.

Wrap your written petition tightly around the Lodestone and place the wrapped Lodestone in the bottom of a potted plant that can survive and thrive in an office environment. Try to avoid using a plant that requires a lot of sunlight if your office space doesn't get any sun. There are plenty of plants that are perfect for an office space; research what's best for your environment by asking someone at your local garden center. You may want to prepare two plants and keep one at home as a "spare" in case the first one shows stress from lack of light. Once your plant has been re-potted with the Lodestone in the bottom, anoint the base of the pot with Crown of Success Oil.

Buy a simple desk toy. It can be a little squeezable stress ball or a wind-up walking robot, but the classic executive desk toy, known as "Balance Balls" or "Newton's Pendulum," is also highly suitable for this kind of an altar. Dress the desk toy with Crown of Success Oil, and as you do so, speak aloud your intention and desire for a promotion.

Place the dressed and loaded potted plant on your desk or in your cubicle along with the toy, which should be leaning against or touching the potted plant. Start your altar to work by encouraging your co-workers and boss to play with the little toy or to enjoy the flourishing plant at your desk. Let people pick up and play with the toy as often as they want to. This way you can offer it to your boss or co-workers when they are having a tough or stressful day. Every time they touch and use the toy they will be adding to your rise in the business, feeling gratitude towards you, and helping you to get one step closer to your desired promotion.

CANDLE MINISTRY ALTARS

A rootworker who maintains a candle ministry has at least one altar set aside as sacred or sanctified space. Many ministers who offer candle services have several candle altars for varying conditions and purposes. For example, at Missionary Independent Spiritual Church in Forestville, California, there is a love and reconciliation altar, a reversing and cursing altar, a blessing and healing altar, and a money and gambling altar. The candle services offered at Four Altars Gospel Sanctuary in the Joshua Tree, California are arranged in a similar fashion. This method of organization is perfect for a candle ministry because a candle for almost any condition can easily be placed into one of these four categories.

For my own candle services I separate the work into three categories. I have one altar for love, one for money and success, and one for Reversing, Uncrossing, and Healing. If I offered cursing for clients, then I would add a fourth altar.

Catherine Yronwode describes how one old-time Spiritualist's altar looked: "One of the best workers i knew placed all of his spells for clients on an old-fashioned built-in wooden carpenter's bench in a room in the back of his candle shop, which had obviously at one time been a carpenter's shop. He had everything on the one altar. He kept things on different parts of the workbench, not all mixed together, but there were no clearly demarked 'territories' on it. I never questioned him about whether having only one altar was a bad idea or not, because he obviously knew his business."

Most candle ministers use glass-encased vigil candles when setting lights for clients. Some set their vigil lights on granite slabs, but most use iron candle stands. A simple way to organize glass candles is to use a metal wine rack laid on its side to space the candles apart and keep them safe.

Don't assume that setting lights is a simple act. It is a powerful form of magic and one that deals with flammable materials. You need to know what you are doing and give the process the focus and attention that it deserves. Glass-encased candles can break, crack, or even shatter explosively. No matter how many candles you have burning at one time, make sure that you are always careful and vigilant with them.

If you would like to know more about candle services or starting your own candle ministry in the Spiritual Church tradition, read:

"The Art of Hoodoo Candle Magic" by C. Yronwode and M. Strabo

FREQUENTLY ASKED QUESTIONS

The Lucky Mojo Forum was begun in 2008. Averaging 60 posts per day, it is an online community in which questions are answered daily about the practice of hoodoo and the use of Lucky Mojo spiritual supplies. The Forum is open to all, and anyone can join and ask questions. The Lucky Mojo Forum can be accessed online at:
Forum.LuckyMojo.com

Answers to questions, be they in the form of advice, encouragement, clarification, or spell suggestions, are provided by both forum members and a dedicated team of moderators who are all graduates of Catherine Yronwode's Hoodoo Rootwork Correspondence Course.

Read more about the Hoodoo Rootwork Correspondence Course at:
LuckyMojo.com/mojocourse.html

The Frequently Asked Questions and the answers that follow have been selected from the voluminous body of information on the Forum regarding traditional hoodoo practices and is intended to complete and augment the information that is included in the preceding pages. Here you will find answers to some of the most commonly asked questions in the forum regarding hoodoo altars and shrines. If a question you have regarding hoodoo altars and shrines hasn't been answered yet, it hopefully will be by the time you reach the end of this book.

When reading the answers to the questions provided, note that usernames followed by an (M) are people who are or were at one time Forum moderators. Those marked (M, AIRR) are moderators who are also in professional practice as members of the Association of Independent Readers and Rootworkers:

Catherine Yronwode	Miss Michaele	ConjureMan Ali
Miss Phoenix	Aura Laforest	Miss Bri
Professor Porterfield	Khi Armand	Devi Spring

These AIRR members can be reached for personal readings, magical coaching, candle services, and custom spell-casting at the AIRR web site:
ReadersAndRootworkers.org

• **Do I need an altar at all?**

How important is having an "altar" on which to work? I'm from the South and was raised around Baptists my whole life, both Black and White, and I can't imagine any of the Black Baptists I've known even considered having a place they referred to as an "altar" or "spirit altar," seeing as how home altar spaces aren't really a part of Evangelical Protestantism. Is it satisfactory to simply have a place where you can set a light?
— Catholic_conjure

I think you may be a bit confused about what an altar is. An altar is merely a surface dedicated for spiritual matters. This does not mean that your altar needs to a table with arcane runes, weird symbols, and strange curios. It can be, but it can also be as simple as a table with a few candles on it.

Altars aren't just a "hoodoo thing," but have existed in the South for a long time. Protestant, Spiritualist, and Catholic Christians maintain surfaces which they decorate with pictures, and where they set up religious iconography and light a candle or two. I've seen these frequently even in the homes of non-practitioners. They may not consider or call it an altar, per se, but it certainly serves a similar function and these "sacred" areas are treated specially.

If you have the room, set up a surface dedicated to your work, if not then create temporary areas, for example using the top of a counter then putting away your materials when not in use, leaving the counter free.
— ConjureMan Ali (M, AIRR)

The concept of an altar is not always called an altar. We use this word nowadays as a convenience, but i have seen these sacred spaces referred to by names like "my family memory place," "my old photos," or by the type of furniture being employed as an altar surface: "the mantelpiece," "on top of my nightstand," "the chiffarobe," "my dresser," and so forth.

I knew one church lady who kept her altar on top of her upright piano. The altar cloth was a piano scarf, and there were framed easel photos of her family members up there. She didn't call it an "altar" and i never saw a candle actually burning, but several candles were in use as "decorations."

Check out Gordon Parks' 1942 photos of Ella Watson's vanity-top altar, too; they are online. You will recognize the style, i am sure.
— catherineyronwode (M, AIRR)

- **How does a hoodoo altar differ from a Wiccan altar?**

What is the difference between a hoodoo altar and a Wiccan altar?
— ArchAngel

Wiccan altars vary according to the tradition of Wicca being practiced, and not all Neo-Pagan altars are Wiccan altars, because not all Neo-Pagans are Wiccan. Hoodoo, however, is practiced primarily within a Judeo-Christian framework. Our altars can be working spaces that will vary depending on what we are doing at any given time. Often there will be a place in the home where ancestors are remembered. If we petition saints then there may be statues, flowers, and petition papers. The conjure practitioner does not have a specific set of magical tools (like a Wiccan chalice, athame, wand, etc). Our tools will vary depending on what we are doing and may include glass vigil lights, condition oils, incense, candles, candle holders, incense burners, mojo bags, herbs, and petition papers. Some conjure workers place images at their altar; others won't have any images at all.
— Miss Bri (M, AIRR)

- **Is a hoodoo ancestor altar similar to a Voodoo religious altar?**

1) I've heard that the first altar one should set up in one's home is for one's ancestors, however, I have already set up an altar for the Voodoo lwa Papa Legba, because he opens doors. I don't have an ancestor altar.
2) What would be a good way of cleansing the ancestor space before I create the altar? Holy Water and Florida Water?
3) I'm guessing a white cloth, a plain white candle, a glass or dish of Holy Water, and pictures of relatives for a plain and simple start. What next?
4) Are pictures of living relatives appropriate on an ancestor altar?
5) What types of incenses would one use on an ancestor altar?
6) Do I offer food or drink popular with the family?
7) What about prayers? I was born and raised Roman Catholic, so I am used to the recitation of specific prayers, but I'm open to suggestions.
8) Is it appropriate to combine the veneration of ancestors with worldly concerns, for example, adding money drawing or love drawing to one's ancestor altar? Or should they be completely separate and distinct?
— FredL

1) Voodoo is a religion that literally has nothing to do with African-American conjure of the United States. You could have an altar to any deity you chose, from Papa Legba to Damballah-Wedo and it would have no impact on what i am about to relay to you.

2) We typically cleanse spaces with Chinese Wash. Since most conjures are Protestant Christian, not all of us use Holy Water.

3) This is okay. It is rather Catholic, however, due to the proposed use of Holy Water, and it seems to have Kardecian Spiritist overtones or an echo of Santeria as well, due to the use of Florida Water.

For more on Kardecian Spiritism, please read this web page at AIRR:
ReadersAndRootworkers.org/wiki/Category:Working_Within_the_Spiritualist_Tradition

For more on Santeria and Lukumi, please see this web page at AIRR:
ReadersAndRootworkers.org/wiki/Category:Orishas

Now, as for hoodoo ancestor veneration, you would usually have some mementos of the deceased — framed photos, a pipe, a thimble, bronzed baby shoes, a pot of graveyard dirt, flowers, and candles. Some folks keep the departed one's favourite perfume or cologne on the altar.

You can read more about ancestor veneration in a conjure context and see actual pictures at these AIRR web pages:
ReadersAndRootworkers.org/wiki/Ancestors
ReadersAndRootworkers.org/wiki/Category:The_Dead_and_the_Graveyard
ReadersAndRootworkers.org/wiki/Bwete

4) In conjure, it is quite common to ask the dead to "watch over" the living, thus we place photos of loved ones — especially those who may need watching over — on the ancestor altar, to commend them to the guardianship of the grandparents who have passed.

5) Whatever suits you or the ancestors! They will tell you what they like. Those of Native American descent, for instance, may request Tobacco.

6) Food and drink are popular offerings. So are flowers (real or silk), and candy, and anything they request.

7) Well, if you are Catholic, and your ancestors were Catholic, then by all means say Catholic prayers.

8) Poverty is a strong delimiter of how many altars one can set up. Many folks just have the one altar.

— catherineyronwode (M, AIRR)

* **How should I make a Catholic saint altar?**

How do you set up a saint altar? What colour cloth do you use or does it matter? Is it set up like an ancestor altar with a cup of water and a shot of whiskey? Do you only use the saint candles or do you use coloured candles as well? Do you burn incense? Any particular kind? Or does it matter?
— blackcateyes

It is customary in folk Catholic practices to relate certain saints to certain colours. These are often the colours of their costumes in the most popular holy cards and chromo images depicting these saints. Thus, for example, Cyprian is associated with purple, Expedite with red, Dymphna with green, Michael with red, Our Lady of Grace with blue, Our Lady of Mount Carmel with brown, Saint Anthony with brown, and so forth. White is also acceptable in most Catholic altars, as is yellow or gold, the colour of beeswax, which, at one time, was the only kind of wax permitted in Catholic churches.

If you want to venerate a saint, I would suggest reading up on that saint first in a regular Catholic encyclopedia and then among folk Catholic practitioners of the culture to which you are an adherent. Note that the folk-Catholic practices of France differ from those of Germany — and all of the European variations differ in turn from South and Central American practices. In the United States you will see a lot of variations, because immigrants have come here from all over the world, and those who are Catholic may have brought to America a wide variety of favourite saints or favourite practices for venerating them or favourite beliefs about their patronage.

Cultural variation does NOT mean that colour, offerings, date of veneration, area of patronage, and so forth "don't matter" — in fact, to many people, these nuances and their cultural origins matter a great deal.

If you are coming to Catholicism as an outsider, i would suggest that in order to gain a coherent, workable view of the matter, you should make friends with someone who was born into the culture which attracts you, and learn how to follow that culture's preferences.

I can't describe all of the many Catholic variations — there are simply too many of them — so, rather than try to generalize, which is impossible, i ask you to read the Lucky Mojo Forum threads named after the saints in whom you are interested and ask about each saint in his or her own thread.
— catherineyronwode (M, AIRR)

- **Which ancestors belong on an ancestor altar?**

Over the years I have learned that many in my family don't have the warmest feeling towards me because of my adoption. I learned shortly after my mother passed that my favourite Aunt had NO love for me at all. I know that my mother and father loved me dearly. I have a picture of them on my altar. My father's mother didn't think my parents should have adopted. But her husband always treated me well. Should I put pictures of my deceased relatives on my altar, regardless of their feelings while living? They are the only family I have. Also I have included pets. They loved me and this I am sure of. And I figured I needed all the love I could use when it came to someone watching over me.

— EbonySmiles

You don't have to have all of your deceased relatives on your ancestor altar. Keep the people who loved you and cared for you on your altar. If you only end up having five or six people on your altar, then so be it. Do not put ancestors who did not like you on your altar. This includes people who were physically or emotionally abusive.

If you have deceased relatives who did not like each other, make separate altars and keep them apart. The altars do not have to be large but make sure they are equal in quality and offerings. Having ancestors who did not like one another on the same altar (in the same room) can work against you as well. If the deceased had an issue that was not solved before they died, then be careful about placing them on your altar. Be careful about putting murderers, child molesters, people with mental disorders, etc., on your altar.

— theredc6

Many folks don't know who their ancestors are at all. Your ancestor altar doesn't have to be for specific people, but can include all those whose blood runs in your veins going all the way back to the beginning of time.

— Miss Phoenix (M, AIRR)

If you are uncomfortable with the idea of having someone who disliked you on your altar, i say don't do it. Like you, i have found it valuable to include my dead pets on my altar.

— nagasiva yronwode (M)

• **How does an ancestor altar differ from a working altar?**

I have used at the same candle altar for several years, but now I am thinking of building a permanent ancestor altar. How do they differ?
— crown

An ancestor altar is almost universally regarded as a "non-working" altar. Spells are not performed here, even in situations where ancestral aid is called upon. Rather, it is a place to commune and connect. However, in the Espiritismo tradition, you may cleanse yourself by verbally petitioning your dead relatives to help while running your hands down your body through your auric field and flicking energetic debris toward the altar. A splash of a perfume on the hands before cleansing in this manner is traditional.

Many folks tend their ancestor altar once a week, refreshing the water glasses, replacing food and offerings, putting out new candles, and spending time in meditation with their ancestors by sitting before the altar after giving prayers of thanks and making requests. Others tend the altar daily.
— Khi Armand (AIRR)

• **Do I need to cleanse my altar between spells?**

After I complete the charm and dispose of whatever is left, do I need to cleanse the altar table I use before I begin next?
— justv

I find that it depends on what you are doing work-wise. If you are doing some harsh or compelling magic then I would cleanse my altar in between uses. I personally am a fan of Van Van or Chinese Wash followed by Hyssop Oil and Psalms 51 if I have been doing Compelling, Reversing, or Revenge jobs.
— Miss Bri (M, AIRR)

I am a big fan of cleaning up after my work, and I feel that it is never a bad idea to take a little extra time to clean your magical space. You don't have to spend all day going through this process, but if you are asking the question if a cleansing is needed, it usually is.
— Miss Phoenix (M, AIRR)

• **How do I cleanse an altar properly?**

I got that you are supposed to use Florida Water to clean your altar. Could I use Holy Water or Chinese Wash instead? Do you wash down everything on the altar, or get a little spritz bottle and just spritz everything with it? I bought Chinese Wash and have it in a spritzer bottle already with some ammonia all ready to cleanse!!! :)
— Blackcateyes

Whoever told you that "you are supposed to use Florida Water" to clean an altar is dumb. Many surfaces are damaged by alcohol, and that's what is in Florida Water.

Want to take the finish off your antique varnished table-top? Florida Water will do it!! Florida Water is ALCOHOL and alcohol will remove 19th century varnishes. Alcohol will also take the paint right off your charming hand-painted Tibetan end table.

If your altar is marble and you cleanse it with vinegar or lemon juice — guess what? You DESTROY your marble altar top. Your cute little Louis XV style marble-top nightstand would be RUINED if you attempted to clean it with vinegar.

If you have an altar cloth on your altar, how is Florida Water gonna help you? It won't! You will have to take the cloth off and launder it in soap and water. DUH! Wash your lovely antique embroidered table-runner cloth with pure soap and water only.

Unless someone knows what the surface of your altar is made out of or covered with, they have no right, rhyme, or reason to tell you what you are "supposed" to do. That idea is a JOKE.

Please, folks, use the good sense that God gave you and that your mother tried to teach you.

Don't let internet idiots lead you on a lock-step march to stupidity!

Ammonia may not be safe for everything you wish to clean.

Chinese Wash cannot be "spritzed" on things straight: it must be diluted in water for use. Prayed over with the 23rd Psalm, it has a long history of use as a spiritual cleaning product because it is mild and safe to use on most surfaces that can be wetted — but you may need to rinse anything you wash with Chinese Wash, because it is, after all, a liquid soap product.

— catherineyronwode (M, AIRR)

- **Do I need to have large altars for my spells to succeed?**

I've seen some great pictures of altars and I notice that some are very large or there are multiple altars throughout a person's home. I'm planning to set up a small altar in my room because it's the only private area of my home. Is that okay, or does the set up and area of your altar affect the spells?

— V

It is common in hoodoo to have an altar in the bedroom, often on the top of the bureau drawer or nightstand. I have never heard any conjure practitioner speak a negative word against this practice. There are other religio-magical systems in which this is forbidden, but they are traditions from other cultures, and thus not relevant to African-American hoodoo per se.

Another common place for an altar is in the living room, where photos of ancestors and distant family may be displayed, candles burned, and vases of flowers placed, both decoratively and with magical intent.

Sometimes newcomers to rootwork who follow a non-Christian religion in which such restrictions apply try to bring their own religion's rules into hoodoo, along with a measure of frowning disapproval for how we practice. The truth is, such intrusions are irrelevant at best and impolite at worst, and when it comes to conjure altars, there are many methods and styles of work, and very few practitioners pay attention to outsiders' lists of "thou shalt nots."

— catherineyronwode (M, AIRR)

When I first started in hoodoo I lived in a very small space and used my bedroom for all of my altars. The top of my dresser was divided — half was for love and half for money. A small table functioned as a general working altar where I dressed candles, wrote petitions, and did jobs for other people. My ancestors and their offerings were on the working altar too. My husband and I slept in that room. We were never disturbed by the altars and he actually found them comforting. Furthermore, my rootwork was not affected by the placement of these altars. Using your room for your altars is fine.

— Miss Bri (M, AIRR)

If you spend a lot of time in your room, it would actually have a positive impact because you could spend more time focusing on your spells.

— Miss Phoenix (M, AIRR)

• **Do I need a separate altar for each type of magic that I am doing?**

I never realized that there could be altars for each subject; i.e., a love altar separate from a money altar. I just have one altar for everything I do. Is that a bad idea?

— chyanna

Some people have an altar for one kind of activity and a separate altar for another kind. That's fine but not everyone follows that route. I for one have one altar I use for all my work. Just keep in mind that you should probably clean it between different jobs. If you just cursed an enemy you should definitely clean the altar, both physically and spiritually, before doing say, a love spell, you know? Hope that helps.

— Turnsteel (M)

Most folks don't have the space to have altars for each condition all over the place. Most of the time what you find in hoodoo is that an altar isn't something fancy, but just a simple space that is dedicated to doing spells, whatever they may be. You will find that many professionals have several altars, but this isn't common for the home practitioner.

Personally, if you were going to do some serious cursing I would keep that separate from other rootwork that you might have going on, but that's just me. And I would make sure to thoroughly clean that space before doing other work in the same place.

It would be a blessing to have the space for that many altars!

— Miss Phoenix (M, AIRR)

I have two altars.

The altar in my room is for conjure and it's served me well so far. I keep it undecorated and plain, except for candles from time to time. I store all my supplies under the table or in a closet I have devoted to such use.

My second altar is in a separate room that functions as a magical temple. This is required for my high magick and ceremonial magick.

Hoodoo is about working in the here and now. In ceremonial magick the focus is on transcendence or otherworldness. My idea is to not mix these two magico-religious systems.

— ConjureMan Ali (M, AIRR)

• **Can I set lights for different situations all on the same day?**

I am getting Road Opener, Break Up, love-related, and business-related candles. Can I set all of them at the same time on my altar, or do I have to light them and petition saints or spirits once I have finished with the first one and so on? And if so, in which order would I light them?

— emmagal

Yes, you can set them simultaneously; however, depending on what you are trying to do, Wednesday is a road opening day, Saturday would be the best day for the Break Up spell, Sunday is an overall success day, Thursday is a day for wealth and expansion, and Friday is for love and money.

Many people work by days of the week, the time of the day, or the Moon. Many also have written that if you need to start immediately, do so. Write your petition, set it under the dressed candles, light the candle and focus on your petition. If you are ordering a vigil candle for a saint, the prayer for that will be included on the label. There is typically a place for a petition within the prayer.

— Miss Tammie Lee (M)

Your candles are: "Road Opener, Break Up, love-related, and business-related." Some would light them all at once on one altar. I would not.

At Missionary Independent Spiritual Church, we have four altars, and your selection happens to work out to one candle per altar. Our altars:
• Blessing: positive changes, health, protection, court issues
• Removal: hot footing, revenge, cursing, dispersal, and damnation
• Love: attraction, drawing, sustaining, marriage, return, reconciliation
• Money: attraction, drawing, business, jobs, career success, gambling luck

So i would light one candle on each altar, with the Road Opener coming first. If you wish to work by the days of the week, which would mean that you light each candle on a different day, either at the same altar or on different altars, you do not need to have seven altars, one for each day of the week. You can have four altars, or even just two altars — one facing East for attraction, and one facing West for removal. If you can only put up one altar, due to space considerations, you can divide it into either two halves or four quadrants, as you wish.

— catherineyronwode (M, AIRR)

• **Is it okay to have sex in the same room as my altars?**

My altar is in my bedroom, where I frequently have vigil candles burning for Catholic saints and for positive aims. Are there any issues with having sex in the same room as your spiritual activities?
— thegoldman

A lot of people have an altar in the bedroom. However, personally, I do not want to keep an ancestor altar in my bedroom or perform sex in front of that altar. I have not heard this about Catholic saint altars, but I would assume that it must be the same case for you. Of course you'd think the saints would know to turn away during such an intimate moment.
— ConjureMan Ali (M, AIRR)

My husband and i keep four altars in our bedroom, one of which is a family blessing and ancestor altar, and we have no trouble having sex in their midst. We do not do any cursing work on these bedroom altars, however.
— catherineyronwode (M, AIRR)

There are many people who will not keep any altars in their bedroom for just that reason. Covering the altar or otherwise blocking it from view with a room divider may be an option for you. I never feel comfortable with altars in sight of the bed, unless I was doing love or sex work.
— Devi Spring (M, AIRR)

This is a really personal issue. In my case, if it were an ancestor altar and there were pictures of my grandparents staring at me the whole time, that might not be something I wanted, but other than that it's not a problem.
— Miss Phoenix (M, AIRR)

Both cultural and personal choices inform the placement of ancestral altars. Some say that they should never be erected in the bedroom due to issues of sexual propriety. Others feel no such modesty and set theirs on the bedroom vanity or dresser. Some say that the kitchen is best because the dead want to be included in the daily conversations and activities of descendants. Others prefer the inviting formality of the living room fireplace mantelpiece.
— Khi Armand (AIRR)

• **Are mirrors okay on a hoodoo altar?**

I have a built-in buffet that is the right size, shape, and location for an altar, however the back of it is a fixed mirror. My instinct tells me that it would not be a good place to operate. Can anyone comment on this? It may be possible for me to cover the mirror with fabric, although I'd rather not.
— Seph

There is nothing wrong with conjuring on furniture that has a mirror behind it. I, for one, use the top of an old dresser with a mirror attached.
— Turnsteel (M)

On the wall above one of my altars is an old-fashioned wood-framed mirror that has been consecrated. As I work at this altar, I look up into the mirror and use it to scry upon my targets to keep track of the spell's progress.
— ConjureMan Ali (M, AIRR)

It really isn't a problem to use the buffet as an altar; in fact it sounds great. However, if you don't trust the space, you won't feel solid about your results. Cover the mirror with fabric or paper if that makes you feel more comfortable.
— Miss Phoenix (M, AIRR)

• **How can I keep my altar discreet?**

I am thinking of using my fireplace mantel in the living room as an altar. On the mantel I have photos of grandparents who are passed away and rosary beads around the photos. Everyone knows I love candles and there are always candles up there. Will this succeed? I want to keep it discreet.
— LEARNING719

It sounds like you have created a lovely altar that is discreet already. Candles are a great form of work and most people won't think anything of it.
— Miss Phoenix (M, AIRR)

Making altars on fireplace mantels is extremely common and popular in the practice of conjure. Being "discreet" is your choice.
— catherineyronwode (M, AIRR)

• **How can I keep my candle altar spells private and secret?**

I am constantly having to move my projects around due to people in my house. I hate this, and I absolutely hate to put out candles. The fact of the matter is I have to hide it. Is there anything I can do?
— elbee

Is there an extra closet that you can lock and use as an altar space? If so, you can always tell people that the space is locked because you put a bunch of hazardous stuff in there to keep away from the baby or the pets.

Or put some religious pictures onto a altar space and ask people to respect your prayer space and not blow out any prayer candles that may be lit.
— Devi Spring (M, AIRR)

To keep my magic private, I use unlabelled, plain candles, set up in my den. I have read that some people rent small storage units for spells.
— jwmcclin (M)

Use four-inch candles that burn out in two hours or less. Keep your supplies in shoe boxes; one for candles, one for oils, one for incense, one for baths and herbs. Set up a little space on a dresser and tell everyone that you would appreciate it if people would leave your things alone.
— Mama Micki (M)

It is traditional for conjures to have a couple altars and I know many who have three or four. Now, you might be thinking, "That's great; I ask about hiding and I get advice to make *more* altars!" but if you are a little sneaky you can keep your spell going and camouflage it in the open. A little table with pretty green plants, a tasteful framed image for prosperity, and green candles is no longer an "altar," it's a pretty table with plants, a picture, and some candles for decoration.

I know a woman whose love altar is the mantel of her fireplace. She had images of herself and her husband, items that have sentimental and magical significance to her, and pretty red and pink candles for "decoration."

Drawers and cabinets for supplies are handy for organization, but the altars can be easily kept in the open with a little ingenuity.
— Miss Bri (M, AIRR)

• **How do I set up an altar in a military barracks?**

I want to set up an altar but I've run into some problems. I was looking into taboos and the way my room is set up violates a lot of altar beliefs. I live in army barracks and we are not allowed to have anything that heats up, so I cannot get incense or candles. I have mirrors, plants, bowls, and some stones. My altar will have to lie above my study area as I share a room. The corners are sharp and high and it is across from the toilet. Which apparently is just a no-no. It's also not in the appropriate direction.
— duckturnrot

In my experience (and personal practice), altars don't have the strict requirements you seem to feel that you have to adhere to.

On a practical level, maintaining a formal altar in an army barracks is likely an exercise that will bring you little besides frustration. You can surround your personal space with such items as bring you devotional comfort, but some type of portable altar would probably be more useful than a large, free-standing one. You can include substitutes for items that you either can't find, or aren't permitted to have.

When you have your own space, build the altar you want. Until then, get by with the altar you need.
— Doctor Hob

Most hoodoo practitioners have altars if they can, but if you can't burn candles or incense, just set up a place with spiritual pictures, statues, and other things that are meaningful to you.
— Mama Micki (M)

For generations, hoodoo has been practiced by people who lived in small or shared quarters. It sounds like you didn't "know" that sharp corners were a "bad idea" until someone told you so.
— MissMichaele (M, AIRR)

A soldier's life can be a difficult one that requires flexibility to get what one needs done. Use the space you have, or see if you can use space in your footlocker, or perhaps make a pocket or matchbox altar.
— ProfessorPorterfield (M, AIRR)

• **Can I mix different spells on one altar?**

I am curious to know if on my altar I can have a series of conjures going for different purposes? I have a very limited amount of space and I have been hesitating to do destructive spells because I didn't want the intents to "mix." For example, I assume it is "safe" for candles for positive aims to be near each other on my altar, but should I quarantine the candles for negative or destructive activities to a separate space?
— Brother_Brad

You can definitely have more than one type of candle on the altar at a time. Doing magic in a limited space isn't just common, it's practically traditional.
— Miss Phoenix (M, AIRR)

First, if you feel like separating your jobs according to the intention, then keep in mind that an altar doesn't have to be a dresser- or table-top.
- You can just as well burn a dressed candle away from other candles by putting it on a little wall shelf or sconce.
- Some folks burn negative candles on the back of the toilet, a faint echo of the days when they would be burned in the outhouse and then, partway through the burn, knocked into the human waste below.
- Some folks burn candles (of any type) in the bathtub, especially when they're not home; this improves fire safety, too.

Second, not every spell is a candle spell. That is, you do not need to conceive of all of your activity as being confined to a candle altar space.
- Are you coercing the doll-baby of a thoughtless or reluctant lover? Keep it in your underwear drawer between sessions.
- Are you using a vinegar jar to break up a couple? Shake it, don't burn a candle on it. Hide it away between sessions.
- Are you blindfolding a doll-baby to keep someone unaware of your efforts? Keep it in a black bag in the closet.
- Do you need to sweeten a family member? Wrap your herbs in your petition paper and tape it to the bottom of your sugar bowl.
- Do you want your sweetening work — say, an Apple spell or honey jar — to keep humming along quietly in the background for months or years? Put it under a plant in your garden next spring.

— Miss Michaele (M, AIRR)

- **Can I burn reversing candles at the same time as money candles?**

Is it true that you cannot put a money candle near a reversing candle, because it reverses the work and your money will leave instead of come in?
— redacepilot

Whoever told you that sure does not practice in the same hoodoo and conjure tradition that i do. All the fear-mongering just sounds stupid to me.

I would try to make two altars, but if i only had the one altar, i would divide it into two parts, the east side for drawing and the west side for removal.

But if i am living in a small place with room for only one altar and my li'l ol' altar is too small to divide into two parts, and i need to burn ten candles for ten things on that one altar, i have been taught, and i know how, to dress, prepare and pray over each candle for the results i desire and require.

Ever been to a Spiritual Church prayer service, where all the congregants get candles and put their own wishes and prayers on them? All those candles go on one altar, and they don't cancel each other out or mess each other up!

So whoever is teaching you that a Reversing Candle will adversely affect a Money Drawing Candle is clearly someone who was never poor, never lived in a small home, and never attended a Spiritual Church prayer service — and, frankly, you need a better and more adept teacher. No lie.
— catherineyronwode (M, AIRR)

- **Can I do a Break up spell and a Love Me spell on one altar?**

Can Love Me and Break Up be done at the same time on the same altar?
— impjnmn

For daily separation, it is customary to do Love Me in the morning, as the clock hands rise, and Break Up at night, as the clock hands fall.

To do the spells sequentially, the Love Me spell is done during the waxing moon, whereas the break up work is done during the waning moon.

Two cloths can be put down — black for the Break Up and red for the Love Me. This is useful for catching all the remains for burial.

Directional orientation is not essential, but it does matter. You could do the Love Me spell facing eastward and the Break Up facing westward.
— aura (M, AIRR)